THE SALSA BOOK

Jacqueline Higuera McMahan

Book Design by Robert McMahan

The Olive Press

Requests for permission to make copies of any part
of this work should be mailed to:
THE OLIVE PRESS, P.O. Box 194, Lake Hughes, Ca. 93532.

Book Design: Robert McMahan
Chile Drawings: Robert McMahan
Tortilla Drawings, Deborah Bowden

LIBRARY OF CONGRESS CATALOG CARD NUMBER
No. 85-63671

ISBN: 0-9612150-8-9 (paper bound) revised

THIRD PRINTING, FEBRUARY, 1991

Printed in the United States of America

Previous books by Jacqueline Higuera McMahan

California Rancho Cooking, 1983
The Salsa Book, 1986
The Red and Green Chile Book, 1987
The Salsa Book, New and Revised, 1989
The Healthy Fiesta, 1990

To Roberto
who learned to taste first
and eat second

CONTENTS

CHAPTER III TORTILLAS, ENCHILADAS, AND OTHER TEMPTATIONS

CHAPTER IV SALSA RELISHES

CHAPTER V   BEANS AND BARBECUE SALSAS

CHAPTER VI FRUIT SALSAS

CHAPTER VII SALSA TECHNIQUES   149

CHAPTER VIII CHOCOLATE ENDINGS AND CHOCOLATE FOR BREAKFAST

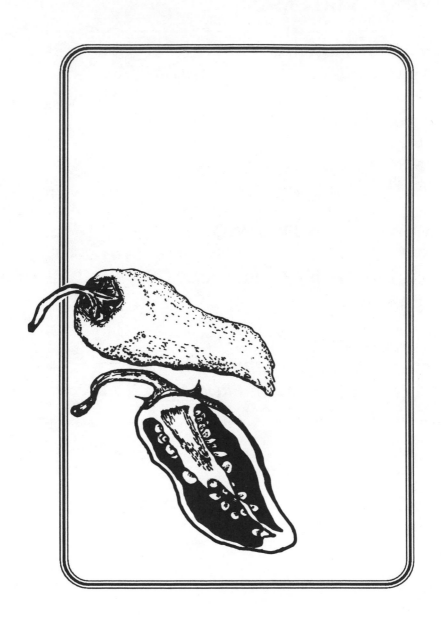

ACKNOWLEDGEMENTS

More than anyone, I have to thank my husband Robert for loving my projects as much as his own and patiently teaching me to trust my word processor, never once laughing at my Dark Age pronouncements. And his palate deserves a medal of valor for being able to forge through months of jalapeños.

My sons, Ian and O'Reilly deserve a thank you for adjusting to the siege known in our household as The Book. I know that they are longing to be the chief tasters for a dessert book.

There is nothing like having someone who believes in your budding ideas and I thank Liz Johnson, who relished the idea of this book from the moment of its inception and never stopped pointing down the road and over the next hill. Thank you Liz for issuing forth the battle cry.

I thank the Huntington Library of San Marino for it was within the quiet reaches of the Special Reading Room, Rare Book Section that I found inspiration over time-worn pages.

To my Mac computer for never faltering, especially during the period of my apprenticeship, I offer my humble thank you.

Computer specialists like Bill Gibson and Jimmie Dow of Computerland have provided expertise and time toward forging new techniques in making books as have the staff at Adobe Systems Incorporated, particularly Ann Robinson. Our gratitude goes beyond these pages.

I thank my father for keeping my knives sharpened, growing enough garlic for my own Garlic Festival, and for not even blinking when I told him I needed 40 pounds of New Mexico chiles roasted when any other person would have run out the back door.

I thank chiles for bringing light into our lives and your lives when you begin cooking salsa.

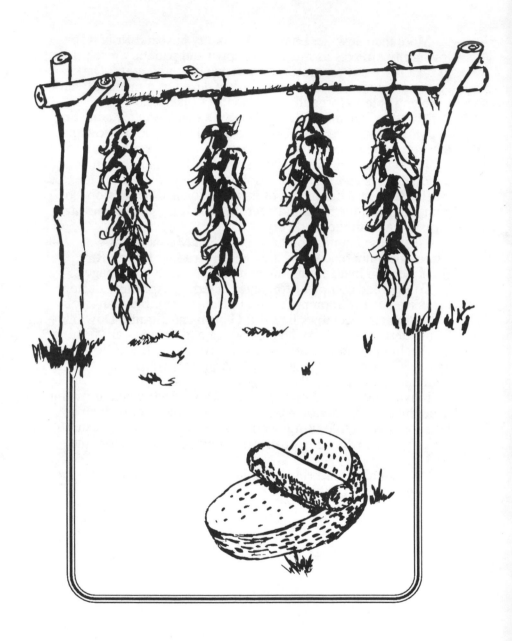

INTRODUCTION

The pungent seeds for this book were sown a few decades ago, when in early childhood I was given my first bite of a flour tortilla dipped into the familial bowl of salsa, without crying out in pain. My mother's family had been in California for eight generations and for much of that period, chile had been a staple on their rancho. Because I did not recoil at hot tamales and red enchiladas, my grandfather proudly assumed the genetics were intact.

When I began work on this book, it was to be a tiny booklet on one of my favorite subjects: salsa. It could probably stretch to 50 pages, I thought, but instead, as I began exploring the world of salsas, I opened up a delicious Pandora's box. Because of favorable timing, the season for chiles and tomatoes was just beginning. At all times, my ice box had at least 20 pounds of three or four types of chiles in the vegetable bins and the shelves were lined with salsa of every hue and kind. My sons complained that there was no room for catsup and tuna and things that normal people keep in their refrigerator. My husband, who at the start just liked salsa, became inconsolable if there were not a half a dozen salsas to choose from for his evening snacks. He eats salsa like some people eat popcorn.

My experiments were concocted around chiles available to everyone through supermarkets, local vegetable stands, and home gardens. As the chile season came to a close in November, my recipe testing had just about been completed also. Then all the chiles turned fire engine red and I could not resist bringing more chiles home by the carload. I placed glass bowls of red jalapeños on the dining table, the snack bar, and kitchen counter. My sons reminded me of child labor laws as I had them threading red chiles onto fishline so we could hang them from the rafters. I have never been taken in by the fake green jalapeño jelly so I began making pepper jelly using the brilliant red chiles and red bell peppers, tossing in chile seeds for good measure. Red chiles are simply the ripe version of the green chiles that are normally available. They add a sweetness and color to your salsas and they can only be found in the late autumn months. In New Mexico, when the green chiles turn brilliant red they string them into ristras and hang them under rafters to sun and air dry for later use during the long winter.

After devoting months to the exploration of salsas, I came out of my kitchen to find that the world had been wildly rediscovering chiles and falling in love with salsa. At this moment, there is a full-scale movement toward chile madness.

Historically, our appreciation is nothing new. When Christopher Columbus brought back chile seeds from his explorations in the New World, chile was accepted immediately as a substitute for costly and rare black pepper. And then it was recognized by botanist-physicians for its medicinal value. According to the documents of ancient herbalists, capsicum has been prescribed for a long list of maladies from toothaches, sore throats, yellow fever, spring fever, and for languid people who need something to make the fire of life burn more brightly. One thing is for sure: the more you have, the more you want.

One old herbal book advised the reader to take a dose of chiles instead of whiskey for the blues and we have found no better antidote for bad days than curling up with a good bowl of salsa. Salsa is cheering, low in fats and calories, high in fiber and best of all, it makes good use of chiles.   To borrow part of a favorite M.F.K. Fisher phrase, a good batch of salsa "will keep the wolf from the door."

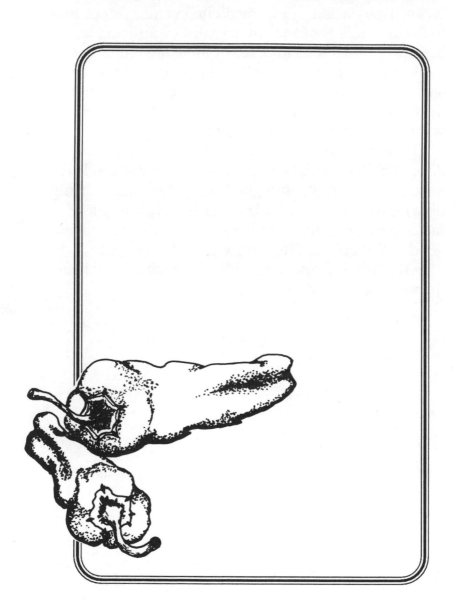

SALSA PRIMER

In working with the ingredients of salsa, there are certain rules of thumb which when followed will make it all sccm easier and perhaps, the mystique surrounding chiles will be lessened. Chiles are really friendlier than they seem.

1. Chiles are the most important ingredient of salsa. There is nothing worse than a bland salsa or a salsa without chiles because you then have just tomato sauce. *Viva chiles!* Truly, when you are worried about hotness, add the fewest amount of chiles, and then taste test, working up to a greater number of chiles.

2. Use superior ingredients. From June to October, ripe, red tomatoes and chiles off the vine are available. There is nothing to compare to a hand-chopped salsa using garden fresh ingredients. Presently in California, there is a renaissance of great vegetable stands. Now we have available a large choice of unusual chiles like poblanos and pasillas, which were impossible to find a few years back.

3. During winter months, use the best canned ingredients. I keep my larder stocked with Italian

plum tomatoes, fancy or premium stewed tomatoes, and the imported tomato puree sold in sealed box containers. For texture, certainly not taste, I add a couple of pink, supermarket tomatoes to my winter salsas with their base of canned tomatoes.

4. A standard home blender is not recommended for chopping salsa for by the time all the ingredients are minced, the salsa is too liquidized, unless that is what you like. Also, be careful not to overprocess ingredients in a food processor or the salsa will appear to be aerated and pink. The excess water in tomatoes causes this to happen. Restaurants making large batches of salsa often use an industrial food grinder. I still prefer hand chopping my ingredients for a fresh salsa as both the texture and the bright color are far superior to a processed salsa. If you are using canned, stewed tomatoes or plum tomatoes (well-drained) for a winter salsa, you can get away with chopping them in the food processor. The cooked tomatoes do not turn pinkish and bubbly.

5. To add that magical touch to their cooking, many Latin cooks toast some of the ingredients such as some of the spices and the chiles. Be careful when you are toasting dried chiles since they burn easily and then the result is a bitter flavor. Toast the chiles in a heavy skillet over medium heat just until the chiles start to soften and give off a whiff of toasty, chile fragrance. Toasting in the oven is risky because you cannot see what is happening.

6. Charring chiles, to do or not to do: it is a necessity to char the large green chiles: the California Anaheims, the New Mexico green chiles, and the poblano or pasilla chiles. These chiles bear a tough skin that is indigestible to some people and when cooked, the skin becomes very papery. Once the skin is blackened and charred, it will easily slip off. If there are a few spots left unblackened that is fine and leave little bits of charred skin here and there for flavor. You do not have to be fanatical in removing every bit of skin. Small green chiles such as the serrano or jalapeño have thinner skins and therefore do not have to be charred unless you want a smoky flavor. When you char chiles over a flame, especially on a barbecue grill, the blackened skins will give your salsas a richer, slightly smoky flavor especially if bits of the burnt skin are left on the chile and blended into the salsa. But when I am using 1 or 2 jalapeños in a salsa, the flavor gain in charring the chiles is so minuscule, I don't bother.

7. When are chiles really hot? Follow the maxim that the smaller the chile and the more pointed its tip, the hotter it will be. The bigger the chile and the more blunted the tip, the milder it will be as with the bell pepper, the milquetoast of the pepper family. You can make chiles less hot by soaking them in salty warm water for an hour. Fiery chiles become hot chiles with soaking. Also, chiles which are chopped and sauteed

in oil become much less *picante* . The most effective step to take in lessening chile heat is to carefully cut along the wall of the chile to remove the placenta or veins containing the volatile capsaicin oil. You can spot the veins by looking for an orange or yellow streak. The capsules containing this oil, not the seeds as is the common misunderstanding, are what make the chile hot. Rub shortening on your hands before working with chiles and the capsaicin oil will not penetrate your skin. Also, oil, especially olive oil, added to your salsas will help to dissipate the pungency of capsaicin. Personally, I never take any steps to lessen the heat of chiles because I love the pleasure-pain brought on by the capsicum family.

8. Technique is all-important. Many salsas have remarkably the same ingredients but because the technique is varied, the flavors are quite different. For instance, I always simmer my cooked salsas in a large 5-quart open saute pan so the contents reduce and thicken quickly in 15 minutes. If a stockpot was used for the same process, the salsa would become mushy before cooking down properly. Also, before cooking, I try to get as much excess liquid out of my raw tomatoes as possible. The salsa will not have to be overcooked in order to thicken and it will remain fresher in taste. Cut your skinned tomatoes in half horizontally. Hold each half over the sink and squeeze out most of the seeds and juice. Cut all the tomato halves into quarters and place in a bowl. Sprinkle with

1/2 teaspoon of salt and allow to sit for 15 to 20 minutes. More juice will be exuded. Drain the tomatoes in a strainer, saving the watery juice for soups or stocks. Use these tomatoes for your salsas or pasta sauce and you will have cut down your cooking time considerably. Since lengthy cooking destroys vitamins, you have conserved more Vitamin C by eliminating excessive water in advance.

9. The sweet and the salty dilemma: more people are conscious today of cutting back on salt and sugar and yet commercially made tomato sauces and salsas can be heavily loaded with both these ingredients. I call salt, the cheap herb, because of its overkill. While I was testing the salsas for this book, I discovered the wonders of rice vinegar. Its use can almost eliminate the need for salt and it actually removes the acidy flavor of tomatoes when added to salsas. Rice vinegar adds a mellow sweetness as if sugar had been added.

10. Remember that salsa (and all cooking) is a creative endeavor. Even though you may be following salsa recipes, please taste test the results. If you love cilantro, add more than required. If you hate cilantro, make the salsa cruda without it. If you are sensitive to chiles, add the least amount called for and then taste.

SHORT CHILE PRIMER

Because of our current movement toward a new recognition of chiles, there is more than ever before, a better understanding of them. However, I could not resist adding my own opinion, which will be short.

Jalapeño chiles- short and fat. My favorite chile because they are hot with flavor. They are like coming in from the cold, standing by the fire until your face glows.

Serrano chiles- skinny and sharp. These chiles give a quick hit, a flash, a door slamming, a blast of heat. I like these chiles when I have a bad head cold.

California chiles - I cannot not like these chiles who are like old friends, old lovers. Mellow with surprises of heat now and then.

New Mexico chiles - These hearty chiles are from the same matriarchal plant as the Californias but they can be downright fiery for old lovers. They are a passionate kiss.

Pasilla chiles - These chiles are my favorite in the dried form as they add character and sweet richness to any salsa. With pasillas, age carries a depth not found in youth. Like a maiden aunt who used to be a showgirl.

Chipotle chiles - Not to be ignored. Jalapeño chiles, when dried and smoked, are known as chipotles. The flavors of this chile unfold in layers upon your palate. This chile has a complex, exotic taste-memory bringing the taster back in time, perhaps to the marketplace of Tenochtitlan.

PREPARING GREEN CHILES FOR SALSA

It is easier to prepare green chiles for use in salsa because they do not have to remain intact, as they do for a dish like chiles rellenos. Relax and burn your chiles.

Your main concern is to remove the tough, translucent skin found on the large green chiles such as the California, New Mexico, or pasilla before adding them to your salsa. If you are working with the small chiles such as the jalapeños or the serranos, you can dispense with the charring, unless you want the smoky flavor. Unskinned chiles should be minced finely. Some Latins don't even remove the seeds but we'll leave that choice to your fortitude and heritage.

For removing chile skin, my favorite method is to impale the chile on the end of a long fork and hold it over the medium flame of my gas stove. Keep turning the chile until it is blackened and charred. THE SKIN MUST BE BLACKENED or it will not come off easily. If you place the chiles in a paper bag or plastic bag, they will steam, causing the skin to loosen. However, this step does further cook the chile by steaming. When I am in a hurry, I just hold the charred chiles under cold, running water and rinse off the blackened skin and do not bother with the paper bag.

For a very effective and quite dramatic method of flaming chiles, you may use a portable propane torch, the type sold in hardware stores and building supply companies. This method is fast and since the surface of the chile is charred without much heat, the chile remains very crisp. You may also use a barbecue grill or a broiler, both of which provide intense heat so you have to be careful not to overcook your chiles before the skins are charred.

Old California proverb that describes someone in a hurry:
that man must have some chiles roasting.

Parece que aquel amigo dejo chiles tatemando.

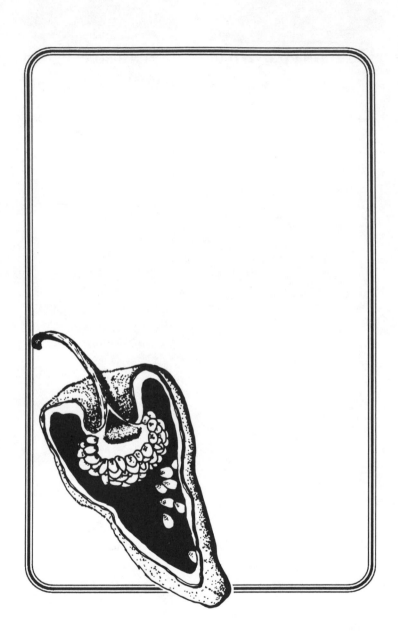

CHAPTER I

SALSAS CRUDAS (Uncooked salsas)

Within this chapter are all the uncooked salsas that are eaten in the fresh or raw state. Many of these salsas are made up of chopped vegetables other than the traditional tomato base. There is the surprise of a carrot salsa that will put ordinary carrot salad to shame and there is a new variation on the green Argentine salsa used with barbecued meats.

Salsa cruda can be either like a sauce or it can resemble a salad. Frequently, it is used as a garnish or side dish for grilled fish or meat.

These salsas, since they are raw, do not keep well past 3 days in the refrigerator. Since freshness is one of their star qualities, salsas crudas should be enjoyed while very fresh.

PICO DE GALLO SALSA

Pico de gallo is a Spanish term meaning rooster's beak and can refer to the Mexican salad of jicama and orange slices or to a Texas-style salsa. Most salsas

served Texas-style have an abundance of chiles. All
the elements of a good pico de gallo should remain
distinct and therefore this salsa never seems to be run
through a blender--when it is done correctly.
Marinated skirt steak or fajitas are usually served with
flour tortillas, grilled onions and peppers, and pico de
gallo.

5 medium tomatoes, diced with skins left on
1/3 cup onion, chopped
2 cloves garlic, minced
2-4 jalapeño chiles, veins and some of seeds
 removed
Salt to taste
Juice of 1 lime
2 ice cubes
3 tablespoons of snipped cilantro (optional)

   Pico de gallo is a time-saving reward to the cook
because you do not have to spend time skinning
tomatoes and chiles so this is the salsa to make after
you raid a country vegetable stand and head home with
a cache of sweet, unwaxed tomatoes.
   Cut the tomatoes in half and flick out the seeds with
a sharp paring knife. Dice the tomatoes into neat
cubes. Cut the chiles in half and remove veins and
some seeds with a knife. Chile seeds, a reassuring trait
for salsa lovers, are frequently found in the salsas of

16

Mexican backwater joints. Mince the jalapeño chiles and add to the rest of the ingredients along with the ice cubes. Due to the hearty amount of fresh lime juice, acting as a preservative, this salsa keep well for three days in the refrigerator.   Add fresh cilantro at the last minute just to the portion of salsa you are serving so the leaves will not turn brownish. Viva Texas!

Makes 3 cups. Serves about 6 people.

CALIFORNIA RANCHO SARSA

Sarsa is the colloquial Old California slang for salsa and the recipe is given here just as it was made up on my family's land grant rancho near San Francisco Bay. Sarsa was prepared fresh a couple of hours before serving and it appeared daily on the table for all meals except tea time or merienda. Breakfast was a groaning board of enchiladas, leftover empanadas, refried beans, huevos rancheros, bolillos, or flour tortillas. We simmer leftover sarsa and serve it on top of our favorite Sunday breakfast of huevos rancheros chased down with cups of thick hot chocolate. Sarsa,indispensable to the smooth running of my household, has been known to cure everything from love sickness to the common cold. It must be hand chopped and the tomatoes must be sun-ripened.

5 ripe tomatoes, peeled, seeded, and chopped
4 Anaheim chiles, peeled, seeded., and chopped
2 jalapeño chiles, seeded and minced
   (canned are acceptable)
1/2 onion, minced
l clove garlic, minced
1-2 tablespoons wine vinegar
2 tablespoons olive oil
Salt to taste
l teaspoon fresh oregano or
   1/2 teaspoon dried oregano
2-3 tablespoons snipped cilantro
2-3 tablespoons tomato puree (optional)

Blister the tomatoes over a flame or plunge into boiling water for 30 seconds and then into cold water. Slip off the skins. Char the chiles over a gas flame or under a broiler until blackened. Place in a paper sack or plastic bag for 5 minutes to steam. Remove the skin under cold running water. Cut off the tops from the chiles and remove veins and seeds.

Combine all the ingredients and allow the sarsa to mellow in the refrigerator for at least one hour before serving. If the salsa seems too thin, you can bind it together by stirring in a few tablespoons of tomato sauce or tomato puree. This salsa keeps well for l day.

If you would like to keep it longer, simmer it for 15 minutes in a saucepan. Keeping power for cooked sarsa is 1 week. It can be used to spoon over huevos rancheros.

Makes 1 quart or serves 6 as a table sauce or 8 for dipping.

SALSA CRUDA MEXICANA

This one could be called salsa rapido because it can be done in a flash by quickly chopping tomatoes, chiles, and onion. My favorite salsa cruda is found in a taco stand in Santa Barbara where all you can buy are open-faced tacos made with hand patted corn tortillas. You take your pile of tacos and Dos Equis beer to a patio where there is a huge bowl of salsa cruda and it is HOT. It has all the veins and seeds chopped right into the salsa but everyone uses it abundantly over their exquisite tacos, including the couple who arrive at the taco stand in their chauffeur-driven limousine.

4 medium tomatoes, chopped
2-3 jalapeño chiles, veins removed along
   with some seeds, minced
1-2 serrano chiles, tops removed, minced with seeds
   intact

19

1/2 cup onion, chopped
1 clove garlic mashed with 1 teaspoon salt
3 tablespoons cilantro, snipped

This salsa should have texture if it is to represent the taco stand properly so hand chop everything. If you promise not to overprocess the vegetables into a puree, you could use the food processor. Just chop using quick on and off pulsations. Stir all of the ingredients together to blend. The beauty of this salsa is its freshness and since it has neither lime juice or vinegar, it should be eaten within a few hours.

Makes 3 cups or enough for 1 person at the taco stand.

AVOCADO SALSA

Do not think of this salsa as guacamole. The avocados must be used at just the right moment in time, meaning that they shouldn't be hard and yet they shouldn't be darkened and mushy. They should just have reached the ripe stage so the avocados can be diced versus mashed. Avocado salsa is the one to beautifully layer over grilled fish filets or boned and pounded chicken breasts or to adorn an open-faced taco. I love this salsa because it presents avocados a little differently.

2 avocados, diced into cubes
2 tablespoons fresh lemon juice
4 tablespoons virgin olive oil
3 green onions, minced (use half of green tops)
2 jalapeño chiles, charred, peeled, seeded, and
*   minced*
2 garlic cloves, minced
1/2 teaspoon salt
4 tablespoons cilantro, snipped

This salsa should not be prepared more than thirty minutes before serving time since the avocado cubes will start to turn brownish. Dice the skinned avocados into neat cubes and immediately cover them with the lemon juice and olive oil. As you can see, this salsa is almost like a dressing. In fact, it also makes a great salad dressing for hearty greens like romaine. Next stir in the green onions, jalapeño chiles, the garlic, salt, and cilantro. Taste to see if you would like more of one of the ingredients.

Makes 2-3 cups or enough for 6 as a garnish over an entree.

CILANTRO SALSA

The universe is divided into two groups made up of those who hate cilantro, poor souls, and my group, the lovers of cilantro. For awhile I was practically alone in my half of the universe and then California cuisine raised our consciousness of cilantro and now it can be purchased in practically every supermarket. This unusual herb, also known as Chinese parsley, can be put into salsas, stews, and in garnish salsas like the one below. This salsa is particularly good with grilled or baked fish.

l bunch cilantro, minced
l/4 cup onion, minced
2 jalapeño chiles, veins and seeds removed, minced
2 cloves garlic, minced
2 tablespoons wine vinegar
3-4 tablespoons olive oil

Combine all above ingredients and allow to marinate for several hours.

Makes about l 1/2 cups or salsa to serve 6 as a garnish.

TOMATILLO ARGENTINE SALSA

This salsa is the best of two salsas, the green tomatillo salsa and the Argentine barbecue sauce with herbs. It is to be eaten cold with tostada chips or bread and is so full of wonderful chunks and spices that it never ceases to demand many helpings. Just as with the traditional chimichurri sauce, this one is good to accompany barbecued meats.

1 pound tomatillos with husks
1/4 to 1/2 teaspoon cumin seeds, crushed
3 cloves garlic, minced
1/2 cup onion, finely minced
1/2 cup pitted green olives, rinsed, chopped
4 jalapeño chiles, seeded, minced
1/4 cup parsley, minced
1/2 cup cilantro, minced
1/2 teaspoon sugar
2-3 tablespoons rice vinegar
1/3 cup olive oil

Using an iron skillet, toast the tomatillos with the

husks intact. Keep turning them until the husks turn brown in spots and the tomatillos begins to soften-about 10 minutes. Allow them to cool completely.

Remove the husks carefully and place tomatillos in bowl of food processor fitted with knife blade attachment. Roughly chop the tomatillos along the all the rest of the ingredients. Do not place large pieces of chiles, herbs, onions, or olives in the processor bowl or you will end up over processing the salsa in order to chop the large pieces. This salsa is beautiful when the character of each ingredient is visible.

Taste salsa and decide if you need a dash more vinegar, olive oil, or pinch of salt.

Makes 3 cups salsa. Keeps for 2 days.

CONFETTI JICAMA SALSA

Most people are unfamiliar with jicama as it is the ugly duckling of Mexican vegetables. It is a sweet root vegetable, the pure white interior covered with a dirty-looking brownish skin. Jicama is best eaten in the raw state and street corners in Mexican villages always have a vendor selling cubed jicama sprinkled with lime juice and chile powder. Many people given jicama plain, end up rejecting it. The delightful salsa below is for those people who thought they didn't like it (like

my husband who loved this salsa but didn't know what
he was eating). This salsa is a refreshing side dish
when you are serving other heavy or *picante* dishes.

1 small jicama (1 pound), peeled and diced
2 carrots, peeled and diced
1 red bell pepper, seeded and diced
1 medium onion, chopped
1 jalapeño chile, seeds and veins removed, minced
2 or 3 cloves garlic, minced
1/2 cup rice vinegar
2 tablespoons light oil
1/4 teaspoon freshly ground pepper
1/2 teaspoon crushed red pepper flakes
1 teaspoon dried oregano
1/4 teaspoon salt
3-4 tablespoons cilantro, snipped

   Dice all of the vegetables into fairly equal sizes.
Using a fork, beat all of the dressing ingredients
together: the garlic, rice vinegar, oil, black and red
pepper, oregano, salt, and cilantro. Pour the dressing
over the diced vegetables and marinate for at least 2
hours before serving.

   Serves 6 as an accompaniment to an entree for lunch
or dinner.

SPICY CARROT SALSA

I have two unofficial food detectives on my payroll (all they require is a hot meal occasionally) and they gave me this salsa as a gift. If you have a friend who is suspicious of hot chiles, start him off on this delicious mild salsa and work up to the powerhouse salsas that call for several chiles.

1 bunch carrots, peeled, shredded
1 small zucchini, shredded
1 bunch green onions, minced using half of the
   green tops
1-2 jalapeño chiles, seeded and minced
1 slice of fresh ginger, peeled, minced
2 tablespoons sesame seeds, toasted
1/3 cup unsalted peanuts
2 tablespoons light oil like sunflower or
   grapeseed oil
1/4 cup rice vinegar
1 teaspoon sugar

Prepare all of the vegetables. Grate the carrots and the zucchini using the shredding disc of a food processor or grate them on a hand grater. Mix the shredded carrots and zucchini with the rest of ingredients. 1 chile makes a very mild salsa so use 2 chiles if you prefer a more *picante* flavor. Cover the vegetables with the dressing ingredients, using the sugar if you think the carrots could be sweeter. This salsa is a delight because it has the wonderful texture of a carrot salad, the kick of a salsa, and the surprise of the ginger and the nuts. This salsa is perfect to serve with sandwiches for a lunch.

Serves 6 as a side to a light lunch.

SANTA MARIA SALSA

In the California coastal city of Santa Maria, they serve a salsa like this one at their famous barbecues. The version given below is a favorite. I have seen this salsa wildly devoured by people who ordinarily eat with good manners. It has a gentle kick so whenever I am serving company as opposed to my fire-breathing family, I serve three gradations of salsas.

Santa Maria Salsa is the mild one at the bottom of the thermometer. This salsa keeps well since it starts off with canned tomatoes and it is best when it has a few hours to marinate. Santa Maria Salsa is meant to marry with a good barbecued steak and a pot of beans.

1 large (1 pound, 12 ounces) can Italian plum
  tomatoes
1 (16 ounce) can stewed tomatoes
1 stalk celery, minced
1 green pepper, minced
2 cloves garlic, minced
1 bunch green onion, minced using half of tops
1 (4 ounces) can flame-broiled green chiles,
  chopped
2 jalapeño chiles en escabeche or regular canned
  jalapeños, minced
1 teaspoon juice from can of jalapeños

1 tablespoon apple cider vinegar
1 teaspoon sugar
Salt to taste
4-5 tablespoons cilantro, snipped

Drain the tomatoes, reserving the liquid for soups or stews. Squeeze out the seeds from the plum tomatoes. Chop the tomatoes and prepare the rest of the vegetables, combining them with the chile juice, vinegar, sugar, salt, and cilantro.

Place the salsa in a glass bowl, cover with plastic wrap, and allow the flavors to steep for at least 2 hours. Keeping power: 5 days.

Makes over 1 quart salsa or enough for about 8 people.

FAST PROCESSOR SALSA

Sometimes you do not have the perfect tomatoes and chiles in your larder nor do you have much time. This fast salsa is the one I make when I have just 5 minutes and we have to have salsa.

1 can (16 ounces) fancy stewed tomatoes, drained
1 handful of rinsed and dried cilantro
3 green onions, cut into 2-inch pieces

1 clove garlic
1-2 jalapeño chiles, seeded

Place all ingredients in the bowl of food processor and mince using short off and on pulsations. Do not overprocess if you want a chunky texture. Stores well for 3 days in refrigerator. Makes 1 and 1/2 cups.

GUACAMOLE SALSA

Guacamole is mashed avocado, known in parts of Mexico as butter of the poor (mantequilla de pobre), but from this point on, we jump into parts unknown. Is there really a recipe for guacamole? This standard salsa is based on the cook's whim but I feel that the cook must first choose the perfect avocados . They must be ripe but I hate the dank, underground taste of guacamole made out of overripe avocados rescued from a forgotten corner of the kitchen. Enrich this guacamole with one of your own homemade salsas and then use it to make the next recipe--the California Layered Salsa.

4 perfectly ripe avocados
1 tablespoon fresh lemon juice
1/4 cup of your own homemade salsa (any kind)
   or storebought salsa

1/4 cup sour cream, plain yogurt, or creme fraiche
1 tablespoon grated onion
garlic salt to taste
1 jalapeño chile en escabeche or regular canned,
  minced jalapeño
1/4 cup cilantro, snipped

Mash the avocados with the lemon juice, using a fork to make a rough texture. Leave a few lumps. Stir in the salsa, sour cream, onion, garlic salt, jalapeño chile, and the cilantro. Now taste and decide if you need to add more of anything in order to suit your cook's whim. Keeping power: none. Serve within 1/2 hour.

Makes about 4 cups or enough for 8 as an appetizer.

CALIFORNIA LAYERED SALSA

This salsa has been called everything in the book and I have had it everywhere in California from elegant cocktail parties to yacht clubs to ladies' club meetings. Some people concoct it totally from cans and bottles and some cooks use only fresh ingredients. Everyone loves this salsa and it can be stunning, depending upon your innate ability as an architect. Otherwise just carefully layer it and enjoy it.

Bottom layer:
l (l6 ounce) can of refried beans with chorizo
  or
l and l/2 cups homemade refried beans

Middle layer:
l cup sour cream
l/2 cup salsa, homemade or storebought
3 green onions, minced using part of green tops

Third layer:
2 cups grated Cheddar cheese

Fourth layer:
2 cups guacamole or half of above guacamole recipe

Garnish layer:
2 tomatoes, chopped
3 green onions, minced using part of green tops
l/2 cup black olives, sliced
A pile of tostada chips

Heat the refried beans to a bubbly simmer and place a 14-inch heatproof platter in a 300 degree oven to warm. Place the beans on the warm platter and begin artistically constructing the layers. Smooth the seasoned sour cream on top of the beans. Next sprinkle the grated cheese over the sour cream. Mound the guacamole in the center of your arrangement so that some of the cheese and sour cream show. Sprinkle the green onions in a ring around the guacamole and in a ring around the sour cream and cheese. Arrange the chopped tomatoes and the olives like alternate spokes on a wheel. Circle the edge of the platter with tostada chips and guests can scoop up whatever layer or layers they like.

Serves about 12 people.

GAZPACHO SALSA

This salsa has everything traditional gazpacho has except it is not soupy. It has crunchy texture, is colorful, and a good picnic salad. I like to prepare all the vegetables and put them in one of those pretty glass containers that can be fitted with a plastic lid. I carry the dressing separately (made at home) and pour the dressing over the salsa salad just before the picnic begins.

Salsa Salad Ingredients:

    6 tomatoes, peeled, seeded, chopped
    l cucumber, peeled, seeded, diced
    l/2 teaspoon salt
    l bunch green onions, minced with half of green
      tops
    l red bell pepper, diced
    l green bell pepper, diced
    l avocado, ripe but still firm, diced
    Juice of l/2 lemon
    l/2 cup cilantro, snipped

Dressing ingredients:

    l/2 cup mayonnaise
    2 tablespoons wine vinegar or fresh lemon juice
    l tablespoon olive oil
    2 cloves garlic
    2 jalapeño chiles (fresh or canned), seeds removed
    a few cilantro leaves
    5 or 6 leaves of fresh basil or l/2 teaspoon dried
    basil
    Dash of Tabasco hot sauce
    l tomato, peeled, seeds removed.
    Garnishes such as black olives, minced parsley or
      cilantro

Chop and dice all of the vegetables for the Gazpacho

Salsa. It is important that you place the tomatoes in a sieve to drain off excess liquid. Salt the diced cucumber and place on a double thickness of paper towels to drain for 15 minutes. Blot with the paper towels and most of the salt will also be removed. Place diced avocado in a small bowl with the lemon juice while you are preparing the rest of the recipe.

You may prepare the dressing by chopping everything with a knife and blending with a fork but I prefer to place all of the dressing ingredients (except the 1 tomato) in the bowl of my food processor. I mince everything together using short on and off pulsations. The 2 jalapeño chiles in the dressing do not cause any fires to start so please add them for their *picante* flavor. When the dressing is whipped together, but not a puree, add the pieces of tomato. Be sure that you blot off the tomato pieces with paper toweling. By following all of these draining and blotting precautions you will be adding the essence of all of the vegetables and not their water. Mince the tomato into the dressing with 2 or 3 quick pulsations.

Stir all of the chopped and diced vegetables together, preferably in a 2-quart glass bowl. Pour the dressing on top to form a creamy layer. Refrigerate for up to 3 hours before serving or carry the salsa to your picnic and add the dressing on the spot. You may garnish the creamy top layer with olives, minced parsley, or cilantro.

Serves 6 for a luncheon or picnic side dish.

CHAPTER II

SALSAS COCIDAS (Cooked salsas)

This chapter includes all of the salsas that are simmered ever so briefly just to take away the rawness and the salsas that are cooked a long time to develop the flavors. As opposed to salsas crudas, cooked salsas can be stored in the refrigerator from 2 to 4 weeks and the flavors are more complex.

SALSA SUAVE

When I began researching cooked, bottled salsas, I analyzed over 20 bottled brands of very mild to fiery hot salsa. I found the two most dominant characteristics to be either saltiness to the extreme or heat and if they were hot, they were hot without much flavor (except salt). I did find one jar of salsa that had great flavor and the recipe for this happy jar of magic is recreated below.

This salsa is so good that we eat it out of the jar, spread on top of thickly sliced French bread, with tortillas, with tostaditos, and we just plain eat it. You can seal Salsa Suave tightly in a jar and bring it on trips. We do. It accompanied us on a holiday trip to Tahiti. Take it in your briefcase to enliven airline flight pablum. Take it discreetly into kindly restaurants to spoon over cheese omelets. The waitress will ask you for the recipe.

4 pounds ripe tomatoes, peeled and seeded,
chopped
4 cloves garlic, minced
2 medium onions, chopped
8 jalapeño chiles, sliced using some of the seeds
2/3 cup apple cider vinegar
3-4 teaspoons oregano
Pinch of cayenne pepper
Salt to taste
2 tablespoons tomato paste

Simmer all of the above ingredients, except the sliced jalapeño chiles, together for 10 minutes to reduce some of the excess liquid from tomatoes. Next add the jalapeño chiles and simmer the salsa for 10-15 minutes longer. I use a large 5-quart open saute pan as it allows the liquid to reduce quickly without overcooking the ingredients. The tomato paste helps to bind the salsa together since fresh tomatoes tend to exude water. This salsa keeps well in the refrigerator for 1 month.

Makes 1 quart.

TOMATILLO SALSA

This lovely green sauce, made with the fruity, Mexican husk tomatoes is one of the natural wonders of classic Latin sauces. The little green tomatoes do not have to be peeled or seeded. Just remove the dry, outer husk. By using the technique given below, you will produce a fresh-tasting, lemony salsa with a gentle, *picante* flavor. My mother-in-law, of Dutch Irish heritage, has resisted hot salsas but she adores this one and has put in her order for a lifetime supply.

1 and 1/2 pounds fresh tomatillos
2 Anaheim green chiles, charred, peeled, and
  seeded
3 jalapeño chiles, partially seeded, veins
  removed
2 cloves garlic
1/2 of a chicken bouillon cube or 1/2 cup chicken
  broth

1/4 cup rice vinegar
1 tablespoon light oil (sunflower or grapeseed)
1/4 to 1/2 cup cilantro, snipped
Pinch of salt

After removing the dry husks from the tomatillos, rinse them well under warm water to remove some of the stickiness. Cut tomatillos into quarters. Cut the Anaheim chiles and the jalapeños into pieces.

To the bowl of a food processor fitted with the knife blade attachment, add the tomatillos, chile pieces, and cloves of garlic. Chop to a coarse puree using on and off pulsations. If you want to use the salsa for dipping tostada chips or spooning onto homemade pizzas or tortas, it is best to make a coarse puree. For a thinner sauce consistency, pulse on your food processor for 20 seconds and puree the salsa. You can further thin down the sauce by adding 1 cup of chicken broth, sour cream, or cream. Stir this liquid in during the simmering stage. This thinner sauce is perfect for enchiladas and tortas.

After you have pureed the ingredients for your Tomatillo Salsa, place mixture in a 3-quart saucepan. Simmer everything, except the fresh cilantro, for 12-15 minutes. Place the salsa into a bowl to cool completely before adding the cilantro. Or store the salsa in a glass jar in the refrigerator for up to 2 weeks and stir a few snipped sprigs of cilantro into the portion you will be serving. Adjust seasonings, such as salt and more cilantro, by taste testing.

This sauce is probably one of the most adaptable of all of the salsas: it can be used for dipping tostada chips; adding zest to guacamole; or saucing enchiladas, tortas, or homemade Mexican pizza.

Makes 3 cups or enough for 12 enchiladas (see Chapter III).

SALSA BRAVA FROM THE MEXICAN CHICKEN PLACE

All over greater Los Angeles and parts of northern Mexico are Mexican chicken joints where they grill chicken which as been marinated in secret tropical juices, spices, and garlic. Everyone has tried to figure out the mysterious marinade for the chicken so I decided to concentrate on the hot salsa they serve in little paper cups.

Everytime I went into the chicken place, I asked a dumb question about the salsa like, "I'm allergic to certain chiles. What kind did you put in this stuff?" That's how I found out the secret ingredient in the salsa was one dried pasilla chile which the counterman said must be toasted first.

And I was duly impressed with the chicken joint in Oxnard when I arrived early one morning to buy chicken for a picnic. The manager was blackening the tomatoes, onions, and serrano chiles over his gas grill. Then I knew that his salsa was for real.

6 tomatoes, charred over gas flame or broiled
  until skin blisters
1 medium onion
1 dried pasilla chile
4 to 5 serrano chiles, charred, skin removed
3 tablespoon cilantro
Salt to taste

Toast the pasilla chile in a heavy skillet until it is softened and releases a toasty smell. Do not burn. If you burn it, throw it out as it will be bitter. When you can handle the chile, break it in pieces and remove the stem and seeds. Place the chile pieces in a bowl and pour in a cup of boiling water. Steep for 20 minutes. Meanwhile prepare your tomatoes by removing the charred skins and squeezing out the seeds. Chop the onion into 2-inch pieces. Remove the charred skin from the chiles but an authentic Mexican joint salsa, must have some of the seed included.

Place the soaked pasilla into the bowl of a food processor with 2 tablespoons of fresh water. Puree for 20-30 seconds. You may also use a blender. Next add the tomato pieces, onion pieces and serrano chiles with some seeds. Roughly puree, using on and off pulsations. If you were working at the chicken joint, you would put in the entire serrano, excepting the stems. Simmer the salsa briefly in a 2-quart saucepan for 10 minutes just to remove the raw flavor. Place the salsa in a bowl and allow to cool. Stir in the cilantro and salt to taste.

Makes about 2 cups for dipping tostada chips or filling soft tacos.

BLACKENED SALSA

This salsa is almost identical to the preceding one except that none of the blackened skins of the tomatoes or chiles are removed, giving a wonderful earthy flavor. This is fun salsa to do when you are barbecuing and can grill the vegetables on the side.

6 tomatoes, blackened over a gas flame or barbecue grill
5 jalapeño chiles, blackened over flame or grill
1 dried pasilla chile, toasted
1 small onion, cut into pieces

2 cloves garlic
Salt to taste

Toast the pasilla in a heavy skillet or over the grill, being cautious that it does not burn. Burned dried chiles are bitter. When you can handle the chile, break it into pieces, removing the stem and seeds. Place in a small bowl and cover with boiling water. Soak for 20 minutes Squeeze out the seeds from the tomatoes. Remove most of the seeds and all veins from the chiles.

Place the soaked pasilla chile into the bowl of a food processor or blender. Add 2 tablespoons of water. Puree for 20 seconds. Next add the tomatoes and all or part of their charred skins, add the chiles, the onion, and the cloves of garlic. Roughly chop so that there are no large pieces remaining.

Simmer the Blackened Salsa in a 2-quart saucepan for 10 to 15 minutes in order to mellow the flavors. Add salt to taste.

Makes about 2 cups to accompany grilled steaks or chicken.

CHIPOTLE SALSA

The chipotles are actually smoked, dried jalapeño chiles. They are hot but with deep flavors that keep unfolding on the palate. If you are a chile aficionado you should know about these chiles already and if you don't, run out and search for them. If Cajun chef, Paul Prudhomme got hold of a chipotle chile, he would never let go.

Chipotle chiles are usually canned in adobo sauce and these would be fine in this salsa.

1 can Italian plum tomatoes, drained
(reserve liquid for soups)
2 tomatoes, skinned and seeded
1 small onion, cut into pieces
2 pickled chipotle chiles (from 7 ounce can)
2 cloves garlic
5-6 green onions, minced
1 teaspoon oregano
1 tablespoon rice vinegar

Break open the plum tomatoes with your fingers and flick out most of the seeds. Cut the fresh tomatoes into large pieces. Place the plum tomatoes, the fresh tomatoes, the pieces of onion, the chipotles, and the garlic into the bowl of a food processor fitted with the knife blade attachment. Using short on and off pulsations, chop the ingredients into a coarse puree.

Place the puree into a 2-quart saucepan along with the green onions, oregano, and the rice vinegar. Simmer for 15 minutes to blend the flavors.

Makes about 3 cups of Chipotle Salsa for dipping tostada chips or serving with grilled meats. This salsa can also be spooned over rock cod or orange roughy during baking.

WINTER SALSA

This salsa could be called winter solace for I invented it one January when only hard, grainy tomatoes a la supermarket could be found. Yet I was craving salsa, not an infrequent occurrence, day or night at any season. I make Winter Salsa all the time in a pinch because my larder is never without canned Italian plum tomatoes and this is the one I make (in a favorite dream) when I am trapped in a well-stocked ski lodge during a snow storm. You see, I never plan on existing without salsa, even during a blizzard. This spicy salsa is also the one we spoon over Huevos Rancheros, our favorite Sunday brunch dish. See recipe below.

1 can (1 pound, 12 ounces) Italian plum tomatoes,
  drained
1 small onion, minced
3 green onions, minced
2 cloves garlic, minced
1 carrot, scraped and minced
2-4 jalapeño chiles (canned or fresh),
  minced , using some seeds
1/2 teaspoon dried oregano
1/2 teaspoon cumin powder
1 tablespoon chile powder (California or pasilla)
2 tablespoons cider vinegar

Slit open the plum tomatoes and flick out the seeds. This salsa is better when it is hand-chopped so using a chef's knife, roughly chop the tomatoes. Add all of the salsa ingredients to a 2-quart saucepan and simmer for about 20 minutes. Taste test to see if you would like to add more of one of the spices. This salsa will keep well for 2 weeks in the refrigerator.

Makes about 3 cups or enough for 6 servings of huevos rancheros or dipping salsa for 8-10 people.

FAMILY HUEVOS RANCHEROS USING WINTER SALSA

On the family rancho, Los Tularcitos, the foundation of Family Huevos Rancheros was always the huge, handstretched flour tortillas, their very size requiring the cook to prepare a large cazuela of salsa. This is the kind of dish that requires the cook to keep everything needed within easy reach. Place each ingredient in a bowl or pan and have them in the order they will be used. Your largest plates should be kept warm in a 200 degree oven ready for action.

3 cups homemade salsa
1 dozen fresh eggs
1 dozen flour tortilla, store-bought or homemade
Light frying oil (I prefer grapeseed or Wesson oil)
1/3 cup melted butter
3 cups Monterey Jack cheese, grated
1 can green chiles, rinsed and cut into strips

Keep the salsa warm in a saucepan. Place 6 flour tortillas on an oiled baking sheet. Sprinkle each tortilla with 1/3 cup cheese. Press a second flour tortilla on top of the cheese. Now brush the top tortilla with a couple of teaspoons of oil or even better, some melted butter. Place these layered tortillas in a 350 degree oven for 10 minutes to melt the cheese and lightly toast the tortillas. Turn the oven down to 200 degrees to keep the tortillas warm and stick in the 6 plates.

Using a nonstick pan and a couple of teaspoons of oil, fry two eggs at a time. Frying time is about 3 minutes for each set of eggs. This is where you have to work better than a Chinese fire drill so everyone can eat together. I use 2 nonstick skillets at the same time.

Place 2 fried eggs on top of one flour tortilla-cheese stack. Smother generously with hot salsa. Sprinkle with a tablespoon of grated cheese and on top of the cheese place a couple of green chile strips. Hold this plate in a warm place while you finish frying the rest of the eggs.

Serve Family Huevos Rancheros with refried beans and more tortillas for sopping up the salsa. This is a great brunch dish to serve to family and friends who like to sit and watch you stand over a frying pan and also a good dish to cure hangovers, sinus headaches, and bad colds.

THE EASIEST SALSA IN THE WORLD

If we get in late on a Sunday after a day of sailing, I stir this easy salsa together and put it over cheese omelets or fast huevos rancheros.

l cup of good store-bought salsa (not too salty)
3 fresh tomatoes, chopped roughly leaving on
  the skins

Simmer in a saucepan for 5 minutes.

Makes 1 and 1/2 cups salsa or enough for for 4 people.

SALSA VERDE

This sauce, used frequently in New Mexico, is called green because of the abundance of green chiles over tomatoes. It is a chunky, all-purpose salsa meant for spooning over enchiladas, burritos, or it can be stirred into a pot of chile, homemade or canned.

2 tablespoon oil
l onion, chopped
6 fresh Anaheim or New Mexico green chiles
  (charred, peeled, seed removed, chopped)

l jalapeño chile, seeds removed, sliced
l pound tomatoes, skinned, seeds removed or l
 can Italian plum tomatoes, drained and seeds
 removed, chopped
2 cloves garlic, minced
2 tablespoons apple cider vinegar
Chicken broth for thinning salsa if necessary
Salt to taste
l/4 teaspoon cinnamon
4 tablespoons cilantro, snipped

Saute the onion in the oil until translucent. Next add the chiles, the tomatoes, garlic, vinegar, salt, cinnamon, and cilantro. If the sauce gets too thick, thin it out with chicken broth until it is the consistency you want.

Makes about 3-4 cups or enough to pour over the top of 8 enchiladas, 8 omelettes, or 8 burritos.

SANTA FE GREEN CHILE SAUCE

There is a lovely small restaurant in Santa Fe, New Mexico, where you can dine inside by candlelight or outside in an overgrown patio that makes you feel as though you were in Old Mexico. I kept asking for more cups full of a fantastic green chile sauce that had been served with my grilled chicken breast. I hinted to our waiter, unfriendly up to this point, that I would like the recipe for the sauce. He disappeared and came back 15 minutes later. Did he ask the chef? He hinted that the chef was out taking in the night air and so he peeked at the recipe. I became very excited at finding out the recipe and the more questions I asked, the more friendly the waiter became. He was an ex-chef and temporary waiter who loved to talk food. He had been waiting on unresponsive customers all evening and was becoming despondent until we came along and asked for a recipe. My guilt at stealing a recipe from a chef taking a break is not as great as my capacity for this salsa.

8 New Mexican or Anaheim chiles, charred, peeled,
* seeded, and chopped*
1 and 1/2 cups chicken broth
1 teaspoon oregano
2 cloves garlic, minced
1/2 cup to 3/4 cups sour cream

This sauce is an example of how good simplicity can taste. In the restaurant, according to our mystery waiter, the green Sandia chiles were pressure-cooked in chicken broth but I have found that simmering the chiles, oregano, and garlic in broth until the liquid is reduced by half, is just as good a technique for the home kitchen. Simmer chiles over medium heat for about 20 minutes. If you are not in New Mexico, you can substitute another type of green chile such as Anaheim, pasilla, or as a last resort, canned green chiles.

Just before serving the sauce, stir in from 1/2 cup to 3/4 cup sour cream to taste. The waiter said it was his job to add the sour cream and that he added the maximum amount for gringos and the lesser amount for natives. I didn't ask how he differentiated between the two, because without asking, we got the hot stuff.

This sauce is good over chicken enchiladas and as the Santa Fe restaurant served it, as a side dish to grilled, pounded chicken breast.

Serves 6 as an accompaniment.

NEW ORLEANS JALAPEÑO SAUCE

It is only fitting that we go from a table in Santa Fe to a table in New Orleans, my other favorite town.

One evening, after dining well in K-Paul's, while I was still polishing off a hunk of pecan-sweet potato pie, a waitress rushed by with a plate of something that looked extraordinary. Why didn't I know about that!? Chef Paul Prudhomme was sitting in his chair by the kitchen door and I implored, "What just went by with that curly-haired waitress?" He smiled as only a guru can and said, "Go back in the kitchen and watch Frank make em but don't ask for the recipe." Chef Paul had been teaching 18 of us at a French Quarter cooking school and had already given us a pack of recipes along with several pounds. Between a blackened redfish order and a rabbit roulade, an order came to Frank for crawfish enchiladas, the object of my curiosity. With his eye on the redfish, Frank grabbed a 10-inch saute pan and got to work with the Jalapeño Sauce and made it up in about 10 minutes. He warmed a couple of corn tortillas, filled them with fresh crawfish meat, minced green onions, some sauce, maybe some cheese-he was moving so fast now it was hard to see stuff flying by. Then he smothered the 2 enchiladas in more Jalapeño Sauce, a waitress grabbed the plate, and something extraordinary went out the kitchen door. Even though I had just finished a piece of pie, I accepted Frank's offer to taste the sauce. Now I had the taste memory to match up with what ingredients flashed into the pan. As soon as I got home to my own kitchen I recreated my version of the New Orleans Jalapeño Sauce.

1 stick butter
1 onion, chopped
2 jalapeño chiles, seeded, minced (more if you like it hot)
1 can Ortega green chiles, rinsed, minced
1 clove garlic, minced
1 teaspoon salt
1/2 teaspoon cayenne pepper
1/2 teaspoon dried oregano
1/2 teaspoon cumin powder
1/2 teaspoon white pepper
2 cups cream, creme fraiche, or 1 cup cream and 1 cup sour cream
Chicken broth for thinning the sauce
3 cups Monterey Jack cheese, grated

Melt the butter in a 12-inch skillet, add the onion and saute until translucent and golden (not brown). Next add the jalapeño chiles, the green chiles, the garlic, all the spices, and the cream. Simmer for about 15 minutes until the sauce has reduced. Cream and creme fraiche thicken beautifully after 15 minutes of simmering but if you are also adding sour cream, stir it in during the last minute of simmering.

Next add about 1/2 cup of chicken broth to smooth out the sauce. You may have to add more if it appears too thick. It should lightly coat a spoon. At the last minute, stir in 2 cups of Jack cheese, reserving the last cup for garnishing your enchiladas. Stir in the cheese just until it melts and remove the skillet from the heat.

I have used this sauce for chicken enchiladas, Dungeness crab enchiladas, and pasta with steamed vegetablles. This sauce is as good as it sounds! So it can serve from 4-8 people depending on whether or not they are homesick for New Orleans.

Makes enough sauce to cover 10 enchiladas.

CHILE CON QUESO RAPIDO

The recipe below is for a fast version of the Mexican hot cheese dip. Everything is heated until bubbly and then served with tostada chips or raw vegetables for dipping. I usually serve it along with one of the salsa crudas so guests can dip from the high calorie to the low.

5 green chiles, charred, skin and seeds removed or
  l can green chiles
l jalapeño chile, seeds removed, minced
2 cloves garlic, minced
l jar (6 ounces) marinated artichoke hearts, drained
l package cream cheese (8 ounces), softened
l/2 cup sour cream
l/2 cup sharp cheese like Cheddar or Kasseri,
  shredded

Chop the green chiles and add to the jalapeño and garlic. Place the artichoke hearts in a strainer and rinse under warm water to get rid of the cottonseed oil. Blot the hearts with paper towels. Chop the hearts and add to the chile mixture along with the cream cheese, sour cream, and cheese.Pour into a l-quart size baking dish and bake in a preheated 350 degree oven for 20-25 minutes or until bubbly. Serve immediately to 6-8 people. I have even stuffed mushrooms with the above mixture. Bake the stuffed mushrooms for 8 minutes at 350 degrees.

MOLE VERDE

This green salsa, with its base of tomatillos, has the complexity of a fine Indian curry of the type handmade on a family grinding stone. The secret is to gently toast the nuts and seeds. Mole Verde, when served in Mexico, is briefly simmered with prebraised pork, turkey, or chicken. It can also be spooned over the top of enchiladas filled with the above meats. I have eaten it over a bowl of steamed rice and been very happy.

1/4 cup blanched almonds
1/4 cup pine nuts
1/2 teaspoon cumin seeds
4 Anaheim or New Mexico green chiles, charred,
  skinned, seeded
2-3 jalapeño chiles, seeds removed
1 and 1/2 pounds tomatillos, husks removed
2 cloves garlic
1 can (14 ounces) chicken broth or 1 and 1/2 cups
  homemade broth
3 tablespoons light oil
1 onion, chopped
1/4 cup cilantro, snipped
1 bay leaf
More broth for thinning mole sauce if necessary

Toast the almonds in a large saute pan for 1 minute. Next add the more delicate pine nuts and stir for 2 more minutes or until the nuts are golden. Do not burn!

Place the nuts and seeds in the bowl of a food processor. Allow them to cool while you work on the chiles. Char the Anaheim chiles, remove the skins, and seed all of the chiles. Hold the tomatillos in warm water and remove the dry outer husks. Cut tomatillos into quarters.

Grind the nuts and seeds coarsely. Next add all of the chiles, the tomatillos, the garlic, and 1/2 cup of the broth. Puree everything together coarsely.

Saute the chopped onion in the oil until translucent.

Next stir in the tomatillo-chile puree and the rest of the chicken broth. Stir in the cilantro and bay leaf. Simmer on very low heat for about 20 minutes to blend the flavors.

Makes about 1 quart of Mole Verde to serve with poached or braised chicken or you can brown some cubed pork loin, add 2 cups water or chicken broth and simmer until tender - about 45 minutes. Stir in the MoleVerde and you will have a very exotic green chile stew.

SALSA DE RISTRA

RED CHILE SAUCE

This salsa is a staple of all Southwestern and Mexican cooking and within our California rancho kitchen, the cook couldn't cook unless she had this red salsa to stir into many dishes. Our classic red enchiladas were always covered with Red Chile Sauce. We used either California, pasilla, or New Mexico chiles which can be store-bought or plucked from your chile ristra as is the custom in New Mexican and authentic California cooking. The dried red chiles necessary for this salsa are found in most supermarkets. The dried California chiles are mild, the pasilla chiles add a rich sweetness, and the New Mexico chiles add fire. Sometimes I add all three types.

> 8 dried red California or Anaheim or New Mexico
>   chiles
> 6 dried pasilla chiles
> 1 quart boiling water
> 3 tablespoon oil
> 3 tablespoons flour
> 2 cloves garlic, minced and mixed with 1 teaspoon
>   salt
> 1 teaspoon oregano
> 1/8 teaspoon powdered cloves
> 2 tablespoons vinegar
> Chicken or beef broth for thinning out the salsa

Remove stems, seeds, and veins from chiles, holding under cool, running water to rinse well. Place the broken pieces of the chiles in a large heat-proof bowl and cover chiles with boiling water. Allow them to soak for at least one hour or more. Keep the bowl covered with foil or a plate but from time to time, shove the chiles down into the hot water, using a large spoon.

Place 1/3 of the soaked chiles into the jar of a blender along with 1/2 cup of the soaking liquid. Blend into a smooth puree, adding more chile liquid if necessary to facilitate blending. But you do not want to add too much water and thin out the sauce. Continue to puree in batches, adding 1/2 cup soaking liquid at a time. Pour this chile puree through a wire strainer into a waiting bowl. Next pour about 1/2 cup of the soaking liquid through the strainer so that you get every bit of the good puree, leaving only the skins behind. Now prepare your roux.

Heat the oil in a large saute pan and next stir in the flour. Cook this roux until it turns a golden color, not brown. Add the garlic, salt, oregano, cloves, chile puree and vinegar. Simmer the salsa for about 20 minutes, stirring frequently. It tends to bubble furiously so watch carefully. Add broth, up to 2 cups, if you wish to thin out the sauce. If you have leftover essences such as juices from pot roast, turkey or chicken, stir these in as they can make the difference between a great sauce and a good one.

Makes about 1 quart Red Chile Sauce for making enchiladas (See page 80), chile colorado, tamale filling, or chile cook-off chile.

QUICK RED CHILE GRAVY

Within the repertoire of all good Southwestern and native Californian cooks is a red sauce that can be made up using a good chile powder so this sauce is as good as your chile powder. Don't use some tired old stuff in a bottle. Incidentally, you can buy good ground chile in cellophane packets usually kept in the ethnic section of your supermarket. The most savory dried chiles are those that are sun-dried but unfortunately these chiles are only available in the fall months.

Also important to the quality of your gravy, is the savory quality of the broth that you use. Save all braising juices from roasting pans and all vegetable juices to add later to your sauces and Red Chile Gravy.

In New Mexico you are always given a choice of red or green sauce over your enchiladas, your stuffed chiles, your burritos, and even your tamales. This Quick Chile Gravy will be quite delicious over any of the above. See recipe in next chapter for New Mexico Stacked Red Enchiladas, page 81.

2 tablespoons oil
l tablespoon butter
2 tablespoons flour
l teaspoon crushed cumin seed
l teaspoon oregano
l clove garlic, minced
1/2 cup chile powder (New Mexico, California, or
  pasilla or use blend)
3/4 cup water
2 cups to 3 cups broth
1/2 cup tomato puree (like Pomi Italian puree),
 optional

Heat the oil and butter and then add the flour and crushed cumin seed. Cook until the flour is a toasty, golden color. Do not brown, which will only lead to bitterness.

Stir in the oregano, the chile powder, and slowly stir in cool water so the chile doesn't lump. Next add the broth. Simmer the gravy for at least 20 minutes to meld flavors. If the gravy appears too thick, add either water or broth. Stir in the tomato puree only if you are a gringo at heart and want to dilute the robust chile fire. Remember though that this action is a last resort for cowards! Actually, it is a good remedy if you did get hold of *picante* chile powder and will assuage the onslaught to your palate.

Makes about 4 cups Quick Chile Gravy to cover 8-10 enchiladas.

RANCHO MOLE

According to several versions of Mexican fables, true classic mole was created a couple of centuries ago by nuns in a convent in Puebla, Mexico when they were being honored by a Spanish viceroy's visit. Mole is one of the fine dishes of Mexico, possessing a complexity not often associated with everyday Latin cooking. When I want to prepare a tantalizing Latin meal, I cook mole.

On the family rancho, the cooks were not fanatical about which chiles were used for mole but it was very important that at least three different chiles be used and at least one type had to be dark. Also, at least two if not three kinds of toasted nuts were ground up and mole would be unthinkable without a round of Ibarra Mexican chocolate. The chocolate will not be evident to anyone except the cook but it will serve to temper the sharpness of the chiles. Taste the mole before you add the chocolate and then afterwards and you will see how magically the chocolate smooths rough edges. Often times when a pot of chile or any red chile sauce is too sharp for me, I will add a bit of Mexican chocolate. Not too much or you will lose the subtlety.

6 dried pasilla chiles
6 dried mulato chiles or 6 pasilla negra (black)
 chiles
4 dried New Mexico or California chiles
4 cloves or 1/4 teaspoon ground cloves
1 piece cinnamon (2-inch) or 1/2 teaspoon cinnamon
6 tablespoons sesame seeds, toasted
  (reserve 2 tablespoons for garnish)
3 cloves garlic, toasted
1/2 cup almonds, toasted
2 tablespoons pine nuts, toasted lightly

1 stale tortilla, torn into pieces, toasted
1/4 cup raisins, soaked in hot water
4 medium tomatoes
  (seared over gas flame or broiled, peeled, seeded)
1 round Mexican chocolate (Ibarra)
3-5 cups homemade chicken or turkey broth

Break each chile in two and remove the veins, seeds, and stems. Rinse chiles off in cold, running water. Place chile pieces in heat-proof bowl and cover with about a quart of boiling water. Cover the bowl and steep the chiles for 1 to 2 hours. From time to time, stir the chiles to keep them submerged. While the chiles are soaking, prepare the rest of the ingredients.

Put the almonds and tortilla pieces in a pie pan and the sesame seeds and pine nuts in another. Place in a 350 degree oven and toast for about 10 minutes. Check after 5 minutes because the pine nuts toast quickly. All the nuts should be a golden color, not browned. After they have cooled, grind the nuts and seeds in a spice grinder until they are finely pulverized. Grind the cinnamon and cloves at the same time. Soak the raisins. Toast the unpeeled garlic cloves in a small skillet. Roast the tomatoes until the skins will easily slip off. Remove all skins, seeds, and excess juice.

Grind 1/3 of soaked chiles in a blender, adding 1/2 cup soaking water. If the chile puree is too thick, add more soaking liquid. When all the chiles have been pureed, pour 2/3 of the puree into a bowl. To the blender jar, add the ground nuts, seeds, and spices, the tortilla pieces, the toasted and peeled garlic cloves, the raisins and their liquid and the tomatoes. Puree the above ingredients and the chile together and then mix it with the chile puree in the bowl. This mixture will be quite thick until you dilute it with broth.

Pour the mole sauce into a heavy 5-quart pot and simmer, stirring frequently while you add the chocolate and 2 cups of broth. You may need to add more broth toward the end of the simmering. Simmer the mole for 1 hour to strengthen the marriage of flavors.

You can make the mole a day or two before you need it as the flavor only gets better. It freezes well or stores in the refrigerator for a week.

Serve mole over the top of roasted or braised chicken or turkey. An alternative manner of serving mole is to brown chicken pieces until golden in hot oil. Place in a heavy casserole pot with a lid (I prefer Le Creuset) and cover the chicken with 2 cups of mole. Bake at 350 degrees for 45 minutes or until the chicken is tender and penetrated with mole sauce. When you get ready to serve your chicken or turkey mole, sprinkle with the reserved, toasted sesame seeds.

Makes approximately 1 quart mole or enough for 2 chickens or 1 turkey.

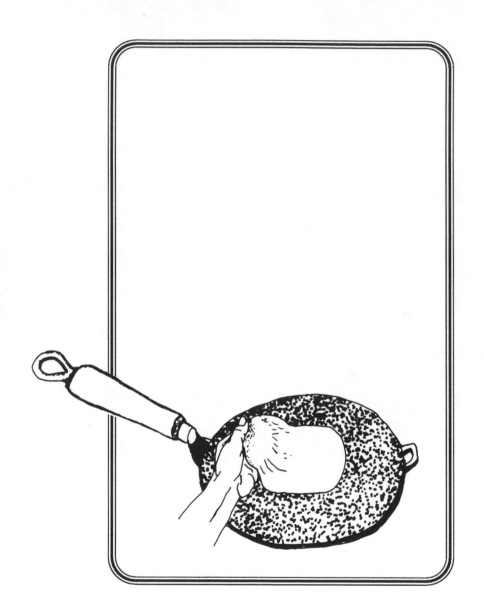

CHAPTER III

TORTILLAS, ENCHILADAS, AND OTHER TEMPTATIONS

Below you will find instructions for the perfect flour tortilla, a variety of enchiladas, and two appetizers using flour tortillas which will give you even more excuses for using salsa.

FLOUR TORTILLAS, THE BREAD OF THE WEST

Popular consciousness probably assumes that sourdough is the bread of the West but in due respect to birthright, flour tortillas came first. Flour tortillas were imported from northern Mexico by the early Spanish settlers. Their great advantage, as a quick bread, was that they could be cooked over a campfire griddle and, when stretched big enough, they could hold an entire dinner in an instantly disposable plate, as the forerunner to the burrito gigantia.

On some of the larger ranchos, granted to Spanish settlers, there would be 5 or 6 flour tortilla makers available for large fiestas. It would disgrace the ranchero to run out of tortillas. My own

69

grandmother, a master of the art, felt that if she always had flour tortillas and a ready pot of beans she could survive floods, earthquakes, and extra guests.

Flour tortillas are made up of the simple ingredients of unbleached flour, a small amount of fat, water, and salt. You will think they are easy after your first attempt if you follow the tips below. You will be rewarded by a taste more delicate than anything you can buy.

Tips for the Perfect Tortilla

1. Use warm water for mixing. Hot water makes the flour granules swell, causing a chewier tortilla.

2. Allow for both recommended resting periods for the dough. It will be much easier to handle. The resting is very important since it will make the difference between a rough dough and smooth, relaxed dough.

3. Place the resting dough in a warm place but not in the oven.

4. When rolling out each tortilla, do not use to much flour The tortilla needs to get a grip on the board.

. - Flatten ball of dough with heel of hand.

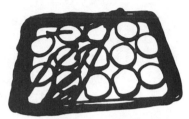

Allow the balls of dough to rest for 45 minutes.

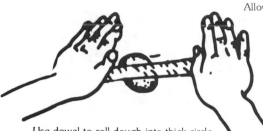

Use dowel to roll dough into thick circle.

Use short, quick strokes. -

Turn the rolled tortilla one-quarter turn. Roll again.

Hold the tortilla on top of the fingertips while stretching.

Push thumb into edge of tortilla to turn

Turn the tortilla several times until no longer puffing.

5. Before rolling your first tortilla, preheat heavy, ungreased griddle preferably of rolled steel or cast-iron. When the griddle is ready, a couple of drops of water will bounce and dance.

6. Do not use a spatula to turn tortillas. Push your thumb int the edge of the tortilla, grab and turn in one swift action of the hand.

7. The most efficient rolling pin for flour tortillas is the palo used by the grande dames of tortilla making. It is a 7-inch dowel or sawed-off piece of an old broom handle. Sand it and clean it before using.

4 cups unbleached, all-purpose flour
2 very rounded tablespoons solid vegetable
  shortening , (l/3 cup)
About l and l/2 cups warm water
l and l/2 teaspoons salt

Dissolve the salt in the warm water and set aside. Using a pastry blender or large fork (I favor an aluminum blending fork from Italy), work the shortening into the flour until it is mealy and there are no powdery remains of flour. Use your fingertips to finish working the fat into the flour.

While you are lifting up the flour with the fork, slowly add the warm water. Drizzle the water into different parts of the bowl. When you have added all but a tablespoon of water, start pushing the dough together. If you feel a dry spot, drizzle in the tablespoon of water. If the dough does not form a soft ball, not too sticky, add water by the teaspoonful but usually 1 and 1/2 cups of water are adequate. Dust the dough lightly with flour and knead for no more than 1 minute.

Wrap dough in plastic wrap or leave on floured board covered with the upside down mixing bowl. ALLOW THE DOUGH TO REST FOR AT LEAST 45 MINUTES TO TWO HOURS. Make sure it does not dry out on the surface.

After the resting period, pinch off 12 to 15 pieces of dough and form into balls. Rotate the ball in one hand as you smooth the edges underneath. Place each ball of dough on a greased baking sheet and, using the heel of your hand, flatten each ball. While you are working keep the pieces of dough well covered with plastic wrap. Allow the dough to rest from 45 minutes to 1 hour. You may refrigerate the dough from 2 hours to one day at this point. Let the dough warm up for at least 1/2 hour before you try to roll out tortillas.

When you are ready to roll tortillas, preheat your griddle over medium heat. Lightly dust your board with flour and place flattened ball of dough in center, keeping the rest of the dough well-covered so it does not dry out. Using a 7-inch long dowel (1-inch diameter), known as a palo, begin rolling the dough into a thick circle. Using short, quick strokes, roll from the center to the edge of the circle. Make a quarter turn of the tortilla after each two short strokes and your tortilla will remain round. By lifting the tortilla up frequently and making a quarter turn, it also makes it easier to keep a round shape as opposed to a violin shape. Violins still taste good.

After you have rolled an 8-inch circle, you may further stretch your tortilla to a thin 10-inch circle. Hold the tortilla on top of the fingertips of one hand while you draw the fingertips of the other hand across the bottom of the tortilla, pulling and stretching in a gentle fashion. Perform this stretching technique twice in each direction to keep the tortilla round. Stretching the dough results in a very thin tortilla akin to strudel and after you try it, you will have fun doing it.

Cook the tortilla on the hot griddle. Keep turning it every ten seconds for about a minute. After you turn it the first time, it will puff in spots, sometimes dramatically, and begin to develop golden spots. Do not push on the tortilla where it is puffing as it is forming layers. This is the difference between your tortilla and the store-bought kind. When you have turned the tortilla four or five times and it is not puffing any longer, it is done. As the old saying goes, "A quiet tortilla is finished." Put your finished tortillas in a piece of foil or wrap in a clean dish towel. If flour tortillas are well-wrapped in a plastic bag, they will keep in the refrigerator for a week. Freshen up tortillas by placing them on a hot griddle and turning until warm and soft again.

You should produce about 15 large tortillas as long as you have not been rolling, cooking, and eating. You will find that tasters, especially children, come out of the woodwork when you are making flour tortillas. The first tortilla, dripping with butter, should go to the cook. One of my favorite childhood breakfasts was to put a flour tortilla, covered with slices of sharp Cheddar, under the broiler until the cheese bubbled and the edges of the tortilla were crisp and golden.

Care of your tortilla griddle: Before conditioning a new griddle (whether cast-iron or rolled steel), wash off residue with hot water and soap. If you want the griddle to develop an antique blackened look then rub it on the top with vegetable oil. Place it directly on medium heat and leave for 1/2 hour. The steel will darken with tempering. To clean a tortilla griddle, scrape off remains of dough or flour with a spatula, run the griddle under hot water, and dry with paper towels. Forever after you must sublimate any puritanical urge to scour your griddle. Scour anything but your tortilla griddle.

TOMATILLO TORTE APPETIZER

You alternate flour tortillas, homemade or store-bought, with tomatillo sauce, Monterey Jack cheese, and slices of jalapeño chile. This appetizer is like a layered Mexican pizza. If you are lucky you might have leftover Tomatillo Sauce from Chapter II (page 39) so you won't have to make up the fresh sauce below. You will need 2 cups sauce for 2 tortes.

8 flour tortillas (4 tortillas for each torte)
1 and 1/2 pounds tomatillos or
 2 (13 oz.) cans tomatillos
1 onion, minced
2 cloves garlic, minced
1 tablespoon light oil
2 tablespoons rice vinegar
2 cups Monterey Jack cheese, grated
1 stick butter, melted
3 jalapeño chiles, seeds removed, sliced
1/4 cup cilantro, snipped
Salt to taste
4 tablespoons Parmesan cheese, finely grated

First prepare the tomatillo salsa: if you are using fresh tomatillos, remove the dry husks while rinsing them under running warm water. Cut them into quarters and place in a food processor. Chop into a coarse puree. If you are using canned tomatillos, you do not have to chop them in the processor. Place tomatillos in a 2-quart saucepan along with the chopped onions, garlic, oil and rice vinegar. Simmer for 15 to 20 minutes. Set aside to cool.

While the salsa is cooling (you may prepare it a day in advance), grate the cheese, melt the butter, and prepare the jalapeños, cilantro, and grated Parmesan.

Preheat oven to 375 degrees F. Place the 2 flour tortillas, which will serve as the bottoms for 2 tortes, on a baking sheet. Brush with some of the melted butter and bake for about 8 minutes or until the edges begin to crisp. Now spread 2 or 3 tablespoons of the tomatillo sauce lightly over these hot tortillas. Cover with 1/4 cup cheese, a sprinkling of cilantro, and a few slices of jalapeño chile. Place another flour tortilla on each torte and brush with melted butter. Cover with more sauce, cheese, chiles, and cilantro. Press a third tortilla on top and brush each one with melted butter. Cover with sauce, cheese, chiles, and cilantro and top with the fourth and last tortilla. Brush each top layer with melted butter and sprinkle each torte with Parmesan cheese. Bake for 10 to 12 minutes until each torte is golden. Cut into wedges and serve immediately. If you have just barely coated the tortillas with salsa, the wedges will not be too messy to eat out-of-hand at a party or picnic.

16 wedges will serve 8 people as an appetizer.

TORTILLA ROLL-UPS FOR PICNICS AND PARTIES

These roll-ups, which you will later cut into pinwheels, are meant for improvisation, so do play with the filling.   I arrange the pinwheel slices on a bed of red leaf lettuce and serve two or three choices of salsa. Salsa Cruda Mexicana and Scorpion Jalapeño Relish are two of my favorite accompaniments to the roll-ups but you can also eat them unadorned and out-of-hand, which is easier if you are at a picnic.

6 flour tortillas (10-inch), fresh and pliable
11 ounces softened cream cheese ,
 (1 large plus 1 small package)
1-2 teaspoons horseradish or
 1 pickled jalapeño chile, minced
1 teaspoon jalapeño juice from can
Pinch cayenne pepper
1/2 teaspoon coarse, grainy mustard
3 green onions, minced (or 2 tablespoons minced
  chives)
4 stuffed green olives, minced
1/2 pound thinly sliced turkey, roast beef, or ham
Tender romaine leaves, slivered
Red leaf lettuce for serving

The cream cheese should be at room temperature so it is very soft and spreadable. To the cream cheese, add the horseradish or chiles, the cayenne, mustard, the green onions, and the minced green olives. Blend well and spread 2 heaping tablespoons cream cheese filling over each flour tortilla, right to the edges. Press about 3 tablespoons lettuce into the cream cheese. Next press thin slices of meat into the filling and to the edges of tortillas.

Now roll up each filled tortilla very tightly. Place each roll on a square of plastic wrap and roll into the plastic wrap, tucking down the edges. Let the roll-ups age for at least two hours or all day so the flavors will penetrate the tortillas. At the picnic site or before serving, slice the roll-ups into pinwheels about 1-inch wide.

Serves about 8 people at a picnic. The recipe doubles or triples easily.

Notes: the recipe above is not written in stone. I sometimes alter it depending on which meat I choose and sometimes I do half with turkey slices and half with roast beef. With roast beef, I may use tiny slivers of red onion and fresh pepper ground over the meat. With ham, I actually have spiked the cream cheese with a tablespoon of my homemade jalapeño jelly. For vegetarian friends, I delete the meat slices and add shredded carrot and 1/2 cup mixture of sunflower seeds and toasted, chopped almonds to the cream cheese.

RED ENCHILADAS WITH SAUTEED ONIONS

These enchiladas, also found in my <u>California Rancho Cooking</u>, are simply my favorite ones. The most likely place they are to be served, is at the table of a rancho family.

3 cups Red Chile Sauce (page 59)
10 large flour tortillas, preferably homemade
4 tablespoons olive oil
5 onions, finely chopped
1 and 1/2 pounds Cheddar or Greek Kasseri cheese,
 grated
1 large can pitted black olives

Cook the onions slowly in hot olive oil for 1/2 hour until they are very soft, but not browned. This step is crucial to the recipe. Stir the onions frequently so they do not stick. The onions will reduce to a thick, sweet marmalade of onions.

Warm the Red Chile Sauce in a wide, flat skillet so you may dip one tortilla at a time into the sauce until it is entirely covered. This is another advantage to these enchiladas. The flour tortillas do not have to be fried first thereby saving you a step plus calories.

Lay the dipped tortilla on a flat dinner plate and place 1/4 cup cheese, 2-3 tablespoons sauteed onion, and 2 black olives down the center. Fold over the sides and gently lift the huge enchilada, with folded edges facing down, to a long, greased baking dish. You will need 2 dishes (12 and 1/2 by 9 and 1/2 inches) or 2 jelly roll pans.

You can assemble Red Enchiladas up to 2 days before you need them. Since they will absorb some of the sauce, sprinkle a few tablespoons of sauce over the enchiladas just before baking in a 350 degree oven for about 20 minutes. During the last 5 minutes of baking time, I sprinkle a little grated cheese on top and stick on a black olive.

I can eat these enchiladas for breakfast, lunch, or dinner. They usually serve 10 people but I always eat two and hide one for the next morning.

RED ENCHILADA STACK FROM NEW MEXICO

In some parts of New Mexico, they favor a layering of tortillas and filling and salsa. It makes a very pretty presentation and what I love about the stack is that you can pile more filling in between the layers. When I am making rolled enchiladas using corn tortillas I always have a struggle with the impossibility of stuffing enough inside the enchilada.

l2 regular corn or blue corn tortillas
2 tablespoons oil
3 cups Red Chile Sauce (page 59 or 6l)
l large onion, chopped, at least l cup
4 cups Cheddar cheese, shredded
3 tablespoons butter
4 eggs
4 green onions, minced
l/2 cup black olives, sliced

Fry each tortilla in a little oil just until softened. Dip each tortilla in some of the Red Chile Sauce to lightly coat. You will need 3 tortillas for each stack, making 4 stacks. As you dip the first 4 tortillas, place them on a greased jelly roll pan. Sprinkle with a tablespoon of onion and 1/4 cup cheese. Fry the next tortilla, dip in sauce, and lay it over the first tortilla plus filling. Sprinkle on more onion and cheese. Fry, dip, and lay on the third and last tortilla. Place the pan of enchilada stacks in a 350 degree oven for 15 minutes. Sprinkle a bit more cheese on top of each stack.
Fry the eggs 3 to 4 minutes in hot butter. Lift each stack, using a wide spatula, to waiting dinner plates. Put a fried egg on top and garnish with the minced green onion and olives.

Serves 4.

GREEN ENCHILADA STACK FROM NEW MEXICO

This recipe makes two large enchilada stacks which are cut into wedges rather than served individually. The idea springs partly from the classic New Mexico stack and partly from a stack of crepes that Julia Child makes.

This is a great way to use up leftover green salsa and leftover chicken.

12 regular corn or blue corn tortillas or blue corn crepes
3 tablespoons oil for softening tortillas
2 cups Tomatillo Salsa or Santa Fe Green Chile Sauce , page 39 or page 52
3 cups Monterey Jack cheese
2 cups shredded chicken (optional)
1/2 cup pine nuts, lightly toasted
1/4 cup cilantro, snipped

Blue corn crepes:

1/2 cup toasted blue cornmeal
2 tablespoons all-purpose flour
3 eggs
1 cup milk
3 tablespoons butter, melted
1/2 teaspoon salt

If you are using either corn tortillas or blue corn tortillas all you need to do is briefly soften them in hot oil. For preparation of the blue corn crepes, beat the blue corn flour, flour, eggs, milk, butter, and salt with a whisk in a large bowl. Using a wire sieve, strain the crepe batter into another bowl. The straining helps to remove lumps. Be sure that you clean off the last remains of batter with a spatula, not losing any of the precious stuff. Stir the batter from time to time as the blue corn tends to settle to the bottom.

Heat a 7-inch crepe pan or nonstick skillet, brush with oil, and pour in a scant 1/4 cup batter. Keep moving the pan and when the top of the crepe looks set, use a butter knife to loosen the crepe around the edges while you are holding the pan to one side of the heat. When the crepe is loose, turn it with your fingers. Cook for 10 seconds longer and remove. As you cook each crepe, stack it between pieces of wax paper. This recipe makes about 12 tortilla crepes.

To make 2 Green Enchilada Stacks, place 2 softened tortillas or crepes on a greased jelly roll pan. Spread with a couple tablespoons of green sauce. Sprinkle each with 1/4 cup cheese, chicken, a couple of teaspoons of pine nuts and cover with the next tortilla or crepe. Continue to use sauce, cheese, chicken, and pine nuts, and tortillas or crepes until you have made up 2 enchilada stacks (6 tortillas each). Cover the top tortilla with more sauce, and cheese. Bake for about 20 minutes at 350 degrees. Garnish with cilantro. Cut each stack into 6 wedges.

CHICKEN FAJITAS
SAVORY CHICKEN FOR STACKS, TACOS, AND BURRITOS

Savory Chicken is so fast and so good you will just want to stand and eat it out of the pan. This is the only recipe in this book in which I am going to be inexact with amounts because it depends on how much chicken you have to cook. I invented this chicken for tacos because the usual boiled or poached chicken does not add enough excitement.

3 or 4 half chicken breasts, boned and skinned, cut into pieces

Home spice blend: use <u>approximately</u> the measurements below for spices. For the spice blend combine cumin, cayenne pepper, thyme, garlic and onion powders, salt, and flour. Increase the spice amounts if you are cooking more than 2 and 1/2 pounds of chicken.

l teaspoon cumin powder
1/4 teaspoon cayenne pepper
l teaspoon crushed thyme
1/2 teaspoon garlic powder
1/2 teaspoon onion powder
1/2 teaspoon salt
l tablespoon flour
2 tablespoons oil
2 tablespoons butter
l or 2 cloves garlic, chopped
l or 2 jalapeño chiles, seeded, minced
1/2 cup to 3/4 cup light beer

This recipe doubles easily but don't try to saute the chicken all at once. After the chicken is skinned and boned, rub it with your home spice blend. If you get inspired, add another spice. Let the spiced chicken sit at room temperature for about 20 minutes.

Using a heavy 12-inch skillet, heat the butter and oil and add l cup of the chicken pieces at a time. Saute over medium heat until golden. Remove to a plate. Saute the rest of the chicken, adding more oil if necessary. When all the chicken is sauteed, drain off any excess oil. Put all the chicken pieces back in the pan, along with the chiles and garlic and add the beer.

A great head of steam will rise up with the most wonderful aroma. Quickly now, clamp on the lid and turn the heat to low. Check every 5 minutes and turn the chicken in the reducing broth. Cook for about 15 to 18 minutes. If the broth cooks away toward the end of the cooking, just add a tablespoon more beer. At the end you should be left with a nice thick glaze. Push the chicken around the beer glaze so it all gets coated. This is about the best taco meat you will ever encounter. Since tacos are filled with other things, the recipe above will serve 4 people unless you ate too much out of the pan.

CHICKEN OR TURKEY ENCHILADAS WITH TOMATILLO SALSA

A couple of years ago I learned an important lesson from Chef Paul Prudhomme while he was philosophizing over a crawfish pie. According to him, each layer of a dish should give a new taste sensation. If you want to create the most delicious chicken enchilada, do not use plain boiled chicken as is often done. Do something special to the chicken. The enchiladas below will give you the Latin version of taste layering!

ENCHILADA FILLING;
Prepare 3 or 4 half chicken breasts (or 1/2 turkey breast) using preceding recipe for Savory Chicken. Set aside while you prepare rest of filling.

2 tablespoons light oil
l onion, chopped
l can (7 ounces) green chiles, drained, rinsed,
  chopped
2 cups Monterey Jack cheese, shredded
l2 corn tortillas
2-3 tablespoons oil

TOMATILLO SALSA
See page 39.   Prepare sauce and set aside.

GREEN ONION SOUR CREAM SAUCE FOR
TOPPING
  l cup sour cream
  l clove garlic, minced
  Pinch of salt
  Pinch of ground cumin
  2 green onion, minced
  l tablespoon cilantro, minced

Using the same skillet you used to saute the chicken, heat the oil and saute just the chopped onion until translucent. Next add the green chiles and saute to blend flavors. Mix the cooled, sauteed chicken or turkey pieces, the sauteed onions and chiles and place in a mixing bowl until you are ready to fill enchiladas.

Combine the ingredients for the Green Onion Sour Cream Sauce. Keep it chilled in the refrigerator because you will not need it until serving time. In assembling enchiladas, it is important to have your fillings and sauce arranged before you on the counter along with 2 long baking dishes.

You should have the bowl of chicken-chile mixture, the shredded cheese, the Tomatillo Salsa and a plate to use for holding the dipped tortilla while you are filling each enchilada.

First soften one corn tortilla at a time by heating it in a nonstick skillet with a couple of teaspoons of hot oil over medium heat. Next lift the softened tortilla to the dinner plate holding some of the Tomatillo Salsa. Dip the tortilla on both sides with sauce. Fill with a few tablespoons of chicken-chile mixture and a few tablespoons cheese. Fold over both sides of tortilla and place the enchilada, seam down, in the oiled baking dish. I cannot make scantily filled enchiladas (they usually get bigger and bigger) just as I cannot make small chocolate chip cookies so I am not one to worry if some of the filling is overflowing.

Cover the filled enchiladas with more sauce and a sprinkling of cheese. Bake at 350 degrees for 20 minutes. Place a dollop of Green Onion Sour Cream Sauce over each serving.

CHAPTER IV

SALSA RELISHES

Within this chapter are all the sweet salsas that can be used more as relishes but they all share one common ingredient. Chiles!

GREEN CHILE CHUTNEY

This sweet salsa has given me great satisfaction because it strays from the garden path, giving the palate something new, and when served at traditional roasted pork or turkey dinners, it adds a welcome change. You're correct if you are thinking that no dinners at our house go unblessed by chiles.

Within the confines of our icebox, milk cartons and mayonnaise jars are pushed into Siberian exile while up front, jars of three or four kinds of salsa line up proudly. My husband most often pulls out this chutney and piles it on top of a hunk of French bread. He says it keeps him from eating dessert.

6 Anaheim chiles, charred
6 jalapeño chiles, charred
6 cloves garlic, thinly sliced

l slice (l-inch) fresh ginger, minced
l tart green apple, peeled, seeds removed, diced
6 cloves, crushed in mortar
  or l/4 teaspoon powdered cloves
l teaspoon cinnamon
l cup brown sugar
l/2 cup sugar
l cup apple cider vinegar

Hold the chiles under cold, running water while removing the blackened skins and seed pods. If you would like a more *picante* chutney, you can reserve some of the jalapeño seeds to include later. Chop the Anaheim chiles and slice the jalapeños.

Place the chiles, garlic, ginger, apple, spices, sugars, and vinegar in a 4-quart saucepan and simmer for about 20 minutes. The sugars will dissolve and the chutney become thicker but you want the chiles and apple to retain texture and not become mushy. Stir the chutney frequently during cooking and do not cook too long or it will become syrupy.

Makes about 2 cups chutney. Store in glass jar in refrigerator. Keeps well for a couple of months.

AUTUMNAL JALAPEÑO JELLY

The urge to make jalapeño jelly always coincides with the migration of birds and whales southward which happens to be the time when bell peppers, Anaheim peppers, and jalapeño peppers are turning red. You can just as well use all green-colored peppers but the flaming red ones will color turn your jars into amber-hued jewels.

At first I hesitated at including jalapeño jelly because there are many other recipes but this version is somewhat different and is included along with some precautionary measures so that you can turn out a beautiful, soft jelly to accompany roasted lamb, pork, or chicken. I stir it into my barbecue sauce and my sweet and sour sauce. The best way to eat jalapeño jelly, other than out of the jar as you stand in front of the icebox, is on top of cream cheese and crackers

1 cup red bell peppers
1/2 cup red jalapeño chiles, red gueros, or red
 Fresno chiles
5 cups cane sugar
1 and 1/2 cups apple cider vinegar, 50 grain
the seeds of 1 jalapeño chile
2 three-ounce pouches of liquid Certo
6 jars (1/2 pint each), sterilized in boiling water
Melted paraffin

Remove stems, veins, and most of the seeds of peppers and chiles. Adding the seeds of one jalapeño chile will not make the jelly hotter since the sugar, the vinegar, and the cooking process tame all the chiles.

93

The floating seeds in the jelly add character. Trust me!

Using the knife blade attachment of a food processor, mince the peppers and chiles with quick on and off pulsations. Alternative method of grinding would be using one of those old-fashioned, cast aluminum meat grinders, fitted with the fine blade.

In a 5-quart pot, mix the peppers, chiles, seeds, sugar, and vinegar. Bring to a rolling boil and boil for 3 minutes. Remove from the heat and cool for 5 minutes. Add the 6 ounces of liquid pectin and stir continuously for 2 minutes. Allow the mixture to cool for another 2 minutes and then stir continuously again for 1 minute more. This stirring will distribute the bits of pepper more evenly throughout the jelly. Without the stirring, the pepper bits tend to rise to the top of the jelly and settle in a layer.

Pour the jelly into the sterilized glass jars or French jelly glasses. Seal immediately with lids that you have separately boiled, apart from the jars, for 5 minutes. Actually I prefer to seal my jelly with a 1/4-inch layer of melted paraffin. Tie a small square of gingham fabric around the top of the jar.

Makes 6 half-pints of jelly.

GLORIA GRAHAM'S CORN RELISH

Corn relish is frequently served in Texas as a side dish to barbecued meats and as a foil to more fiery salsas. If you build up too much heat with Pico de Gallo or Salsa Cruda Mexicana you can cool down with a corn relish. My husband asked me to get this recipe from my friend, Gloria everyday until I got it and then he asked me when I was going to make it every day until I made it. It is the best corn relish.

16-20 ears of very fresh corn, yielding 8 cups cut
corn
4 cups celery, chopped
2 cups green pepper, chopped
2 cups sweet red bell pepper
1 large onion, chopped (1 cup)
2 cups sugar
2 cups white vinegar
2 cups water
2 teaspoons celery seed
1 tablespoon salt
1/4 cup all-purpose flour
2 tablespoons dry mustard
1 teaspoon tumeric
1/2 cup cold water

Husk the corn. Cook in boiling water for 5 minutes. Plunge 5 ears at a time into a large bowl filled with cold water and a tray of ice cubes. Remove the ears of corn. Set aside and cool the rest with the cold water bath. Drain and cut the corn from the cobs. This process is easier if you stand the ear of corn on end in a large bowl. Cut down the cob with a sharp knife and the corn will fall easily into the bowl instead of flying east or west. Set aside the cut corn.

In a 6-quart pot, combine the celery, red pepper, green pepper, onion, sugar, vinegar, water, celery seeds, and salt. Bring to a boil and boil uncovered for 5 minutes, stirring occasionally.

Meanwhile, combine flour, dry mustard, tumeric, and the cold water. Blend with a fork. Now add the flour mixture along with the cut corn to the boiling mixture. Return to boiling, stirring continuously for 5 minutes.

Pack loosely while hot into pint jar, leaving 1/2-inch headspace. Adjust jar lids and rings, which you have simmered in boiling water for 5 minutes to sterilize. Process the jars in a boiling water bath for 15 minutes. Begin timing after the water bath has returned to boiling.

Makes 7 pints.

SCORPION JALAPEÑO RELISH

As I have explored the world of salsas I have adhered to one maxim with singular purpose. A salsa has to have a kick! This particular relish is hot but with flavor. I suspect that this salsa is even hot enough for William Weber Johnson who, after tasting every salsa I have ever given him, proclaims "I could stand it a little hotter." Scorpion Jalapeño Relish is for salsa aficionados but even I was surprised when a couple of my tamest tasters said they would love it on a barbecued hamburger.

5 pounds ripe tomatoes
3/4 pound onions (about 2)
1 cup thinly sliced jalapeño chiles (yes, this is
  correct), with veins and seeds removed
2 red or green bell peppers
A tablespoon of chopped garlic (nothing less)
1 cup apple cider vinegar
1/2 cup sugar (the sugar appeases the cup of
 jalapenos)
1 teaspoon salt
1 teaspoon chile powder
1/2 teaspoon coarsely ground pepper

Drop 5 or 6 tomatoes at a time into a pot of boiling water for 30 seconds. Slip off the skins. Cut in half horizontally and squeeze out the juice and seeds. Chop the tomatoes and onions with a large chef's knife.

Using a 4 or 5-quart saute pan, simmer the tomatoes and onions for about 10 minutes. Then add the rest of the ingredients, adding 1 chile's worth of seeds for added character. Simmer for 20 minutes or until much of the excess liquid is reduced and the salsa has thickened. You must watch carefully here for you want the chiles to retain some crispness and not be cooked to the mushy stage. To prevent over-simmering of the relish, tilt the pan and spoon off some of the watery liquid that collects on the bottom.

Makes 2 pints.

OLD LOS ANGELES CHILE SAUCE

This is the sauce that started me on my search for many, many salsas for while reading an antique cookbook, the <u>Los Angeles Times Cookbook No. 4</u> (1911) with recipes of pioneer, Spanish settlers and families of the dons, I was overwhelmed by the number of salsas native to the West. The Old Los Angeles Chile Sauce is sister to our chile sauce of today except the Spanish cooks added an abundant amount of green chiles versus bell peppers. I have adjusted the amount of sugar and spices of the old recipe but actually I have remained very loyal to the original, down to the last chile.

Old Los Angeles Chile Sauce is good with meats but I most often stir it into homemade mayonnaise, lemon juice, and minced green onions to make dressing for Crab Louis Salads. You can also stir dry mustard to taste into a cup of chile sauce and use it for dipping shrimp.

9 pounds tomatoes, peeled, seeded, chopped,
 drained
1 tablespoon salt
3 white onions, chopped
2 stalks celery, chopped
10 Anaheim chiles, charred, peeled, seeded,
chopped
1 green bell pepper, chopped
1 red bell pepper, chopped
1 and 1/2 cups apple cider vinegar
2 teaspoons cinnamon
1 teaspoon allspice
1 teaspoon cloves
1/2 teaspoon freshly grated nutmeg
1 cup sugar
1 tablespoon chile powder

Mix the chopped tomatoes in a large bowl with the tablespoon of salt. Allow them to sit for 1 hour. Drain them in a colander. With this amount of tomatoes, you will drain off from 3 to 4 cups liquid which you can save for soup. By draining off the liquid now you will not have to cook the sauce for 2 or 3 hours to thicken it.

Simmer the tomatoes in a heavy 6-quart pot for 20 minutes. After the tomatoes have thickened, add the onions, chiles, bell peppers, vinegar, and spices. Simmer for 30 minutes. Stir frequently to keep from burning. Next add the sugar and keep simmering the chile sauce for another 30 minutes or until it is the consistency you like. The sauce should be reduced by one-half from the beginning to the end of the cooking time.

Ladle the chile sauce into sterilized jars. Seal with sterilized lids. Simmer in boiling water bath for 20 minutes. Start timing after the water bath has returned to the boil after adding jars.

Makes about 4 pints.

PEAR - GREEN CHILE RELISH

The first time I served this relish I slathered it onto my homemade French wholewheat bread, layered on some roasted turkey breast, red leaf lettuce, and more Pear-Green Chile Relish. My chief taster proclaimed it the best sandwich he had ever tasted or at least it tied with the New Orleans muffuletta. This concoction is the gourmand's pickle relish, with enough of a hint of chiles to give it real personality.

3 pounds Bartlett pears, ripe but firm
3/4 pound onions
4 jalapeño chiles (1/2 cup), seeded
2 Anaheim chiles, charred, seeded
2 red bell peppers
2 cups apple cider vinegar
2 cups brown sugar
1 teaspoon ground ginger
2-3 teaspoons tumeric for color
2 teaspoons dry mustard
1 rounded tablespoon honey
2 teaspoons soy sauce

Peel and core the pears. Place 1/3 of the pears at a time into the bowl of a food processor fitted with the knife blade attachment. Mince the pears, using quick on and off pulsations. If you do not have a food processor, you can mince everything with a sharp knife or food grinder. Mince all the rest of the pears, onions, Anaheim chiles, jalapeño chiles, and red bell peppers.

Place the prepared pears and the rest of the ingredients in a heavy 6-quart pot. Simmer for about 30 minutes but guard against simmering too long as you want to retain the texture of the pears.

Spoon the hot relish into sterilized jars. Cover with sterilized lids and rings. Place jars in a simmering water bath, bring water bath to a boil, and simmer with lid on for 15 minutes.

Makes 4 pints.

SWEET PICKLED CHILES

The recipe below is an adaptation of "Mary Wallbank's Pickled Chiles" from Helen Corbitt's Greenhouse Cookbook. You can use canned green chiles if you are in a hurry. Sweet Pickled Chiles keep beautifully if stored in a glass jar in the refrigerator and are a good side dish for roasted pork, chicken, turkey, and fajitas. We like them slipped into sandwiches made with a crusty bread.

12 green chiles (Anaheim or New Mexico),
*   charred, and peeled   OR*
*   2 large cans (7 ounces each) chiles*
1 cup white vinegar
1/2 cup sugar
1 teaspoon mixed pickling spice

Cut the chiles into bite size pieces. Simmer the sugar, vinegar, and pickling spices together for 5 minutes until sugar is dissolved. Pour the sweet brine over the chiles. After they have cooled, store them in a quart-size jar. You should mix these up at least 4 hours before serving them.

Makes 1 quart pickled chiles.

PINK PICKLED ONIONS

If you are wondering about the proliferation of everything pickled, it's because an overheated palate, bombasted with *picante* salsas and chiles, seems to be appeased by either vinegar or sweetness. These onions are good if stuffed into a burrito, taco, or rolled up flour tortilla with fajitas or barbecued meat. Guests behave like children at a birthday party when given an array of relishes for stuffing into their tortillas so I usually serve little bowls of the pink onions, pickled chiles, three or four different salsa crudas, and of course some kind of beans.

2 medium red onions, sliced into rings
1 cup vinegar
1/2 cup water
1 tablespoon olive oil
1-2 teaspoons oregano
1 bay leaf
5 crushed peppercorns

Simmer all the ingredients, except the sliced onions, in a saucepan for 5 minutes. Pour this marinade over the onions and allow them to steep for at least 1 hour before using. They will turn a pretty pink color which is the main reason for using the red onions. Stored in the refrigerator, they will keep for a month.

Makes 1 pint.

PICKLED JALAPEÑOS

These chiles are reassuring to me because I know that if I decide to make a salsa or guacamole on the spur of the moment, I can turn to them. This fall I let all my chiles hang on the vine until they turned brilliant red and then I pickled 2 quarts of jalapeños for emergencies. Very few people would eat these straight. If I do not have fresh chiles I mince up a couple of Pickled Jalapeños and add them to a salsa. They are also good when sliced into rings and sprinkled over cheese and bean nachos.

1 quart red or green jalapeno chiles (or mixture),
* about 1 pound chiles*
1 cup water
1 and 1/2 cups white vinegar
1/2 cup mild oil
3 mashed cloves garlic
2 carrots, sliced
1 onion, sliced
2 bay leaves
1-2 teaspoons salt

Char the chiles and place in a plastic bag to steam for 10 minutes Remove the charred skins under cold water, leaving the chiles intact. Do not cut open.

Combine all of the ingredients except the chiles and simmer for 5 minutes. Place the chiles in a quart jar and pour in the hot brine. You will have to spoon the sliced carrots and onions into the jar. The chiles will keep in the brine, refrigerated, for a couple of months.

The brine can be used to season salsas and the carrot slices can be nibbled on. See below for special pickled carrots.

Makes 1 quart of Pickled Jalapeños.

JALAPEÑO CARROTS

These carrots are so popular with everyone I had to include them with all the other marinated vegetables. They are perfect to nibble on with wine and cheese before dinner, serving to tantalize the appetite.

2 bunches carrots, scraped
1 cup apple cider vinegar, white vinegar,
  or rice vinegar
1/2 cup water
1/2 cup olive oil
1 onion, sliced thinly
5-8 canned jalapeño chiles, some seeds removed
1 teaspoon sugar

Buy the freshest, tenderest, young carrots with tops intact. After peeling, cut diagonally into 3-inch pieces. If the carrots are tiny, don't cut them. Leave them whole. Using a steamer basket or a pot with a steamer insert, steam carrots for no more than 6 minutes. The secret is not to overcook the carrots so they remain crisp.

Mix up the marinade of vinegar, water, olive oil, onion slices, and jalapeño chiles in a large bowl so you can dump in the hot, steamed carrots as soon as they are ready. Stir the carrots around in the marinade and then sprinkle the sugar over the top of the carrots. While the carrots are cooling, stir them from time to time.

The carrots get better, the longer they remain in the marinade, but if you can't resist, try one. Keep refrigerated. I store my carrots in a fat 64 ounce jar that once held artichoke crowns. At times, I have put them in more aesthetic jars, stuck in a sprig of cilantro, and brought them to friends as a house gift.

Drain the carrots before serving them on a bed of parsley or cilantro. They are also good when accompanied by sticks of sharp cheese.

Serves 10 as an appetizer.

MARINATED MUSHROOMS

These mushrooms, along with the Jalapeño Carrots, keep my guests happily nibbling while I am still rushing around the kitchen.

l pound very fresh, firm mushrooms
3/4 cup rice vinegar
1/4 cup water
1/4 cup olive oil
2 cloves garlic, mashed
2 dried Japones red peppers
l sprig of thyme or 1/2 teaspoon dried thyme
5 or 6 cracked peppercorns
l teaspoon soy sauce
l tablespoon minced parsley

Quickly pass the mushrooms under cold, running water. Wipe each one carefully with paper towels to remove any grit. In a saucepan, heat the rice vinegar, water, olive oil, garlic, peppers, thyme, and soy sauce until it simmers for a couple of minutes. Cool the marinade down for 2 minutes and then pour over the mushrooms in a bowl. Stir them every once in a while until they are cool. Make at least 2 hours before serving.

To serve, lift the mushrooms out of the marinade and arrange on a dish. Sprinkle with minced parsley.

Serves 6-8 as an appetizer.

GARLIC OLIVES

   This a marvelous way to flavor canned, domestic olives especially if you use a virgin olive oil in the dressing. After these have marinated for a couple of days, they remind me of the garlicky olive salad spread on the New Orleans muffulettas. In order to make this sandwich, you would have to use about 1/2 cup of the Garlic Olives with juices, about 1/2 cup of pickled, bottled Italian vegetables, 1/2 teaspoon oregano, and 1 tablespoon parsley. Chop the entire mixture roughly and then stir in another tablespoon of virgin olive oil for good measure. Unless you are in New Orleans, you won't find the real muffuletta bread but a 10-inch round of French bread or sourdough will do nicely. Drizzle some of the vinegary olive oil and juices onto both halves of the bread, which you have sawed in half. Cover one half with salami and layer in a goodly amount of the olive salad. Now add a layer of provolone cheese and either mortadella or Italian ham. Try to fit on the top lid of bread and press the muffuletta together. Then try to eat without breaking your face. It tastes best if you are sitting on a bench by The River.

1 large can pitted green olives
1 large can pitted black olives
1/3 cup virgin olive oil
2 tablespoons red wine vinegar
3 cloves garlic, minced
3 green onions, minced
1 teaspoon pepper flakes with seeds

Drain the olives of juices and combine with the rest of marinade ingredients. Marinate for several hours or days. Serve as an appetizer or chop up olives a little, mix with some of the marinade and spread on sourdough bread for sandwiches.

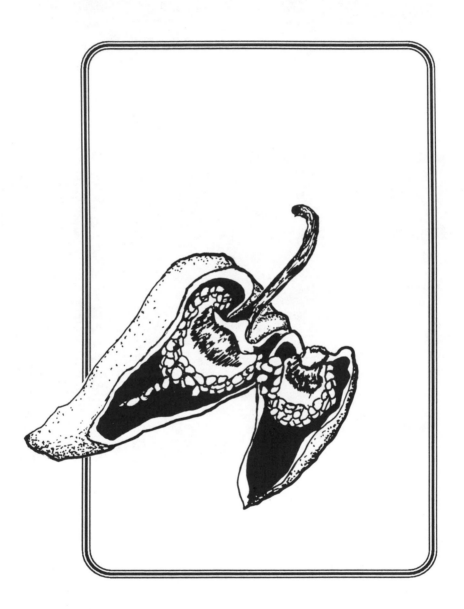

CHAPTER V

BEANS AND BARBECUE SALSAS

During any Western barbecue, beans were and are as important as the meat. Beans have experienced periods of rejection because they were either poor people's food or were fattening but they are now enjoying a renaissance due to our new recognition of the importance of "carbos." And thanks to updated research, it has been discovered that beans can be more digestible by following a hot water soaking method for a 4-hour period and by then throwing away the soaking liquid which contains more irritants than it does nutrition.

It is as difficult to cook a good pot of beans as it is to cook a good omelet. Cooking beans is difficult because most people put them on a fire and walk off, assuming that the beans will cook themselves. Well, they require a watchful cook, lifting the lid, sniffing for any beans sticking to the bottom of the pot, a gentle stir with a wooden spoon, adjustment of the fire, perhaps a little more coarsely ground pepper and thusly you will be letting the beans know who is boss.

My mother and grandmother both cooked highly prized beans but my husband was initiated into my style of bean cookery during our first weeks of marriage when I decided to surprise him with enchiladas and beans. We lived in San Miguel de Allende, Mexico and were struggling students. Down the street from the impressive Banco de Comercio, was the Bean Bank where our meagar funds were kept in a magnificent black and gold safe upon which usually sat a white cat who would jump onto the counter while you were trying to withdraw a 100 pesos. The bank manager also sold beans, these being stored in gunny sacks along the stone-paved hallway. One particular afternoon, along with my pesos, I requested a kilo of pinto beans, which the bank man weighed on antique brass scales.

Upon returning home from the Bean Bank I put the beans on to cook and diligently added an onion and some salt. By the middle of dinner that evening, my new husband had his plate piled with rocks and stones which had miraculously appeared out of my bean pot. I apologized to him. I cried and swore I would never buy beans from the Bean Bank again. The moral of the story lurks not within the Bean Bank but that you must always pick over and rinse your beans with a hawkeye!!

THICK RANCHO BEANS

These thick, flavorful beans are still our favorite. A bowl of these beans is as satisfying as sitting in an old kitchen watching your mother cook while you lean head on hand taking in the fragrances. The secret to these beans is that you do not add an excessive amount of water to the pot, thus diluting the flavors. A common error is to start off with too much water.

1 pound pinto or pink beans
5-6 cups fresh water
1 ham hock or piece of ham bone
1 onion, chopped
2 cloves garlic, minced
2 teaspoons to 1 tablespoon ground chile powder
Salt to taste (added last 1/2 hour of cooking)
Coarsely ground pepper

Rinse the beans in a sieve and diligently search for stones. They frequently are the same color as the beans. Place the clean beans in a 4 quart pot and cover with water. Bring to a boil and simmer for 3 minutes. Turn off the heat, allowing the beans to soak for a minimum of 4 hours.

Pour off the soaking water. You are not throwing away vitamins and minerals, but only substances that can cause digestive problems later (according to the lastest bean research). Add from 5 to 6 cups of fresh water or just enough to barely cover the beans. Bring to a simmer and turn heat down to maintain a gentle bubbling. Add the ham bone, the chopped onion and garlic. Place on the lid so just a whisper of steam escapes. Check the beans every 20 minutes to make sure they are not sticking. Give a stir with a wooden spoon. Keep a teakettle filled with hot water so if the bean liquor looks like it has cooked down, beneath the level of the beans, you can add a 1/2 cup water. The most likely time to add more water is during the first hour of cooking. Never add too much water!

The beans should be tender after 2 and 1/2 to 3 hours cooking. When they are tender add salt to taste, pepper, and chile powder. Simmer another 1/2 hour and then scoop out about 2 cups beans with a little bean liquor. Roughly puree in a blender on low speed. Stir the puree back into the bean pot and cook for a few more minutes with the lid off. You will then have beans thick enough to roll into a tortilla.

Serves 6.

REFRIED BEANS RANCHO-STYLE

There are two things that you need in order to do these beans properly and that is a heavy cast-iron skillet and a pot of thick beans, preferably using the recipe above. Pinto beans make meatier refried beans and pink beans are a prettier rosy color if that makes any difference.

If you are using a properly seasoned cast-iron skillet, you won't have to use as much grease when you are frying. Rather than mashing the beans as you put them in the hot skillet (the way it used to be done) you can ROUGHLY puree them in a blender or food processor but please leave coarse pieces or even some whole beans.

3 or 4 cups well-cooked pinto or pink beans
3 tablespoons oil for frying like grapeseed oil or safflower oil
1/4 cup dry, grated cheese (Romano or California Dry Monterey Jack)

Heat oil in heavy 10 or 12-inch skillet. If the beans are already mashed you may add them to the skillet and press them into a flat pancake shape. After they have sizzled on low heat for a couple of minutes, turn them. They should become toasty around the edges. When they have thickened enough and they are fried to your preference, sprinkle on the cheese and serve. These beans are good to spread on nachos and to serve with huevos rancheros.

Serves 4-6.

PRAIRIE FIRE

The recipe below, adored by everyone, has been adapted from The Helen Corbitt Collection. One evening when I was assembling it while guests were watching from the snack bar, they wouldn't leave it alone. The Prairie Fire was supposed to go with the fajitas but most of it was gone by dinner time.

However, it is perfect to accompany barbecue like fajitas and is good when used as a base for nachos or for just dipping into with tostada chips.

l quart prepared beans (red, pinto, pink)
2-3 tablespoons butter
l/2 pound cheese (Monterey Jack or Cheddar),
 grated
4 canned jalapeño chiles, minced with seeds
l or 2 teaspoons jalapeño juice from can
l/4 cup minced onion
2 cloves garlic, minced

Puree the beans in a food processor. In a pinch, you could use canned pinto beans and they will work well in this recipe. Place the pureed beans and the rest of the ingredients in the top half of a double boiler that contains simmering water. Stir beans until cheese is melted.

To serve, place Prairie Fire in a chafing dish and guests can dip in their bread or tostada chips. Give it a stir every now and then so cheese doesn't stick to the bottom of dish.

Serves l0-l2 as an appetizer.

NORMA'S DRUNKEN BEANS

In the countryside around San Luis Obispo, great pride is taken in lavish barbecues which are always accompanied by several versions of the local pinquito beans. This coastal area is the only place where the tiny pinquito beans are grown. Norma's pinquitos are always the first ones gone at the barbecue.

2 pounds pinquito beans or pintos
boiling water to cover beans
1 ham hock or ham bone
2 onions, chopped
3 cloves garlic, minced
1 bay leaf
1 can beer
1 and 1/2 to 2 cups of tomato puree or Pomi strained
 tomatoes
1 can stewed tomatoes (1 pound, 12 ounces)
2 tablespoon chile powder
Salt to taste
Worcestershire sauce, a dash

Pick over the beans for rocks. Rinse them in a sieve. The night before cooking time, pour boiling water over the beans and let them sit till the next morning.

Pour off the soak water. Place beans in a 5-quart pot and cover with fresh water. Add the ham hock, onions, garlic, bay leaf, and flat beer. Simmer for 2-3 hours or until tender.

119

Remove ham hock and drain off some of the cooking liquid and reserve. To the beans in the pot, add the tomato puree, stewed tomatoes, chile powder, and salt. Add some of reserved bean liquid if beans seem too thick. Simmer together for 20 minutes to blend flavors. These beans are best if made one day in advance so the flavor may blend.

Serves 10-12 at a barbecue.

BLACK BEANS

Black beans, traditional in Latin and Carribean countries, are gaining a following north-of-the border. They are one of my favorites in the bean family and they are especially good to serve with seafood or Cuban-style along with side dishes of sour cream, salsa, cilantro, and small pitchers of rum or sherry so everyone may add a jolt to their bowl of beans.

1 pound black beans (turtle beans)
boiling water to cover beans
1 onion, chopped
3 cloves garlic, minced
1 sprig epazote (optional)
1 bay leaf
1 chipotle chile adobo, canned
Salt to taste

Rinse beans under running water. Pick over for stones. Place in pot and cover with water. Bring water to the boil. Allow the beans to steep in the water for 4 hours. Pour off the soak water (you are not losing any vitamins or minerals) and cover the beans with fresh water. Bring to a simmer and add the chopped onion, garlic, epazote, bay leaf, and chile. Simmer for 2 to 3 hours or until tender. Add salt to taste. You may serve them as is or puree them in a food processor, blender, or food mill as is done in Yucatan, Mexico. If you decide to puree them, drain off some of the liquid and reserve so that your puree is not too watery. Serve the black bean puree with fresh limes or a dash of sherry or rum.

FAJITAS WITH MARINADE

Fajitas, currently the rage in big cities as far distant as Paris, were originally cowboy fare and cowboys know a good thing. Fajitas, as prepared on the Sonoran, Chihuahuan, and Texas ranges by camp cooks were the inner diaphragm muscle of the steer known as the skirt steak. Skirt steak is a little tough, has great flavor, and used to be dirt cheap until becoming fashionable. Since it has become not only hard to find but expensive, I have substituted flank steak. If you can find skirt steak, use it instead of flank if you prefer to be traditional.

The success of your fajitas depends upon your

marinade, lots of good salsa and guacamole, and a stack of hot flour tortillas with which to envelop everything.

1 and 1/2 to 2 pounds flank steak
Juice of 2 limes
2 tablespoons soy sauce
2 tablespoons olive oil
2 cloves garlic, minced
1/2 teaspoon granulated garlic
1/2 teaspoon pepper
1 onion, sliced plus 1 tablespoon oil
2 green chiles (Anaheim or pasilla)

Prepare marinade of lime juice, soy sauce, olive oil, garlic, granulated garlic, and pepper. Cut 4 shallow slashes across the grain of each side of the flank steak. Place steak in a glass dish and pour in marinade, rubbing the garlic into the slashes. Marinate for at least 2 hours at room temperature.

The greatest error committed in the name of barbecuing is placing meat over the fire while the coals are too hot. We have all experienced black, raw chicken from a patio barbecue. The secret is to allow the coals to reach the white ash stage.

Light the coals at least 45 minutes before you need them. We like a combination of good briquets and mesquite. Use an electric starter. Stay away from fluid starters due to the chemical residue. When the coals are covered with white ash, use a stick or tool to tap off some of the ash. Place the grill over the coals and allow it to get hot. Put on the steak. Exact timing depends upon the thickness of the meat. You will need 6 to 7 minutes per side for rare; 8 minutes per side for medium; 10-12 minutes per side for well done. While you are grilling the meat, place the 2 chiles on the edge until they are charred.

When cooked to your preference, remove the steak to a cutting board and cut across the grain making thin, uneven slices. Remove most of the charred skin, stems, and seeds from the chiles. Cut into strips. Saute the onion in a little oil for 2 minutes just to sear. Before serving toss the meats strips, the onion, and chile strips together. In restaurants they pile everything on searingly hot cast-iron plates or griddles.

Serves 6 as long as you have plently of salsa and tortillas.

CHIMICHURRI SALSA

This salsa is a specialty of Argentina where it is served abundantly with their highly prized steaks. Most people upon tasting chimichurri, assume it to be more complicated than it is. It is freshness and simplicity and it happens to be a favorite of my twelve-year old twin sons, staunch members of the pizza and hamburger generation. This pleases me immensely for now I am a little assured that down there somewhere are the taste buds I educated from day one. You should eat Chimichurri Salsa with a good grilled steak.

1/2 cup parsley, minced (about 1/2 bunch)
1 tablespoon onion, minced
3 cloves garlic, minced
1 canned or pickled jalapeño chile, minced
  (the chile is optional but delicious)
2 teaspoons dried oregano
1/2 cup olive oil
1/4 cup vinegar
1/2 teaspoon salt
1/4 teaspoon freshly ground pepper

Most importantly, after washing off your parsley, dry it very well between paper towels or even better, in a lettuce spinner. There is nothing worse than a mess of chopped, wet parsley. Remove the stems and chop the parsley with a sharp chef's knife.

Add all the rest of the ingredients to a bowl and stir in the parsley. Taste test to see if you would like a dash more of vinegar or pepper. Traditionally this salsa is not hot but we all love the jalapeño chile. Chimichurri loses its freshness after 3 days. It is also good with roast beef and fish.

Makes 1 cup for 6-8 people.

124

THE CHIEF BARBECUER'S DUNKED
BREAD

On our family rancho, Los Tularcitos, there could be no barbecue without dozens and dozens of handstretched flour tortillas which were the primary utensil. Once in a while we part from tradition to eat a superior bread and this one is IT. The original recipe comes from Joe Guidetti, a legendary California barbecuer who has cooked for governors and common folk alike and he serves Dunked Bread with all of his barbecue. The trick is the beer because it makes the butter sink in more deeply. We eat salsa on top of the dunked bread.

1 long loaf French bread
1 stick salted butter
1/3 cup beer
1-2 cloves mashed garlic
1/2 cup freshly grated Parmesan cheese

This recipe doubles or triples ad infinitum for big barbecues. The butter and beer are usually melted together in a roasting pan along with the garlic. Cut the bread in half horizontally and then cut 1-inch deep slashes along the length of each half.

Dip each bread half into the melted butter mixture, making sure all the slashes are well covered. Sprinkle with Parmesan. When you are ready to serve the bread, place it on the grill or run it briefly under a broiler just long enough to turn golden and melt the cheese.

One loaf feeds 8.

JEFF COMMON'S SANTA CRUZ BARBECUE SALSA

Jeff invented a great way to use the Santa Cruz Pure Chile Paste from Arizona, made from ripe, red chiles which are hot and sweet rather than having the usual sharpness characteristic of dried red chiles. This recipe is good to baste chicken and ribs on the barbecue when they are almost done.

l jar (2 cups) Santa Cruz Pure Chili Paste
Alternative to chili paste below
l cup honey
l cup soy sauce
1/4 cup dry sherry

If you do not have the chili paste in your pantry when you need it (see address below), you can use 8 dried California or New Mexico dried chile pods. Break up the chile pods, rinsing under cold water while you remove the seeds and stems. Place in bowl and cover with boiling water. Allow the chiles to steep for l hour. Remove and grind with as little water as possible in a food processor or blender.

Mix the chili paste or ground chile puree with the rest of the ingredients. Simmer for 5 minutes in a saucepan to blend the flavors. This sauce is best if made the day before you will be needing it.

Use this sauce over chicken, turkey parts, or ribs. When your barbecued meat is just about done, start basting with the sauce and keep turning the meat or chicken. One of the important things to remember about barbecuing chicken is to stay with it and keep turning. An old bartender I know, who is a master chicken barbecuer, says he turns his chicken pieces 40 times. If you are using a barbecue sauce and put it on too early, it will simply blacken by the time the chicken is done.

Makes 1 quart sauce. Store in refrigerator for 1 week or freeze. Santa Cruz Pure Chili Paste is obtainable by writing to Santa Cruz Chili Company, Amado, Arizona 85640.

TILLIE'S VERY BEST BARBECUE SAUCE

This sauce is rich, tangy and very, very close to the sauces swabbed over chicken and ribs at those great barbecue joints that are always found on mean streets. The trick to Tillie's sauce is to slowly saute the onion until it has become sweet. If you like your barbecue *picante* , add more cayenne and hot sauce and I always add some jalapeño jelly.

4 slices bacon, sliced into 1/2-inch pieces
1 onion, chopped
1/2 teaspoon black pepper
1/2 teaspoon cayenne pepper
1 teaspoon garlic powder
1 and 1/2 cups or 1 can chicken broth
2 cups bottled barbecue sauce (any brand)
1/4 cup light molasses
1 cup honey or use 1/2 honey and 1/2 jalapeño jelly
Juice and sliced rind of 1/2 lemon or lime
Juice and sliced rind of 1/2 sliced orange
4 garlic cloves, minced
1 teaspoon Louisiana hot sauce

Saute bacon pieces until crisp. Add the chopped onion. Cover pan and continue to cook until onions are dark brown but not burned. Stir from time to time to keep them from sticking. This step will take about 15 minutes. Next add the black pepper, cayenne, and garlic powder and cook for a couple of minutes longer to season the onion and bacon.

Add the liquids to the pan in the following order: the chicken broth, barbecue sauce, molasses, honey and jalapeño jelly, the fruit juices and their rinds, the minced garlic, and the hot sauce. Stir well and simmer for 1/2 hour or longer if you wish the liquids to reduce a little into a thicker sauce. Also if you want a thick sauce, you may use one of the thick, chunky barbecue sauces at the beginning. Remove rinds at the end of the simmering. Taste for seasoning. More pepper, more cayenne, more hot sauce, more jalapeño jelly?

Use for brushing onto chicken or ribs on the barbecue grill. And I frequently simmer leftover pot roast, pork, or sausages in this sauce.

Makes about 1 quart, stores well in refrigerator for several weeks.

SALSA BORRACHA

In the outback of Mexico, there are variations of drunken sauce, so called because it includes as much tequila (or pulque) as the cook will give up. Long before thegreatyoungchefs discovered mesquite, Mexican campesinos were squatting over their humble mesquite fires grilling chickens the way they have done for centuries. When my husband and I moved into a small apartment in Queretaro, Mexico, the first thing we did was set up our barbecue grill in the open-air laundry room. We went to great pains trying to light massive pieces of mesquite and basted our chickens with Salsa Borracha to the stupefacation of our Indian maid who spread rumors around the building that the señora cooked like a campesina even though she had a pretty new gas stove.

5 dried ancho or pasilla chiles
2 ripe tomatoes or use 2 canned stewed tomatoes
2 cloves garlic, minced
1/4 of a medium onion
Juice of 1 lime
2-3 tablespoons tequila
1 tablespoon oil
2 teaspoons brown sugar

Heat up a heavy skillet and lightly toast the dried chiles. Keep turning them until they soften and give off a toasty aroma. DO NOT BURN OR TOAST DARKLY or your sauce will be bitter. When cool enough to handle, hold the chiles under cold water and rinse out seeds, discarding along with the stems. Pour boiling water over the chiles and allow to soak for 1/2 hour covered. Place chiles in a blender with a couple tablespoons of soaking water, the tomatoes (skinned and seeded), onion, garlic, lime juice, tequila, oil, and brown sugar. Puree until a thick sauce consistency. Taste to see if you want more lime juice, tequila, or brown sugar. Because they blend well and are ripe, I frequently use a couple of fancy or premium, canned tomatoes instead of fresh ones.

This sauce is great when brushed onto grilling steaks, roasts, chickens, or turkey parts. You can brown turkey filets or sliced, raw turkey breast in a little oil, cover with drunken sauce and bake for 30 minutes in the oven at about 350 degrees.

SPANISH SAUCE, TURN OF THE CENTURY

I found this recipe in an old cookbook with pages so fragile I was afraid to turn them. Within the collection were recipes of Spanish ladies of Los Angeles in the early 1900's. This recipe is testimony to the longevity of a good thing.

The Spanish lady advised that this sauce will keep all winter if bottled and she would take a portion of the sauce and simmer it with minced green onions, minced olives, salt, and garlic and baste her roasts with it or serve it with cold ham, fried eggs, or fried oysters.

12 dried red chiles (California or New Mexico)
2 teaspoons salt
Juice of 3 limes
1/2 cup very mild olive oil

Wash the chiles and break them up, discarding the seeds and stems. Place chiles in large bowl and cover with salt and boiling water. Place lid on the bowl and allow the chiles to steep for 1 hour.

The Spanish lady used a silver spoon and a wooden bowl but you can use a food processor or blender to puree the soaked chiles, using as little soaking liquid as possible to facilitate the process. Push the chile puree through a sieve to remove the skins. Be sure and scrape off all the puree from the bottom of the sieve.

Place puree back in the food processor and add all the lime juice. With the machine on, slowly add the olive oil through the feed tube. Our lady advises that the chile puree and the olive oil should be worked into a mayonnaise.

Makes 2 cups sauce. Stores in refrigerator for 2 months.

ACHIOTE SALSA FROM YUCATAN

One of the staples of the Yucatecan kitchen is achiote, a spicy paste made up of ground annato seeds and blended with vinegar and spices. In the native marketplaces, mounds of freshly ground achiote (adobo) are sold and whenever a friend has made a trip to Yucatan, I have pleaded for fresh achiote. Now it is available from time to time in Hispanic grocery stores and in the Grand Central Market of Los Angeles on 3rd and Hill. It is worth a pilgrimage as once you find it, it will keep for years in the refrigerator if well wrapped in plastic.

In Yucatan pork and chicken are rubbed with achiote paste, the juice of the naranja agria (sour oranges) and spices, wrapped in banana leaves and roasted over grills or in ovens. The meat will have an earthy rust color and the flavor can be compared to no other spice, No substitute here. Pork shoulder prepared with achiote makes great meat for tacos.

4 ounces or 1 package achiote paste
1/2 cup fresh orange juice
1/2 cup rice vinegar
1 heaping teaspoon oregano
1 heaping teaspoon cumin seed, crushed
Pinch salt
1/4 teaspoon ground black pepper
3 cloves garlic, minced
2-3 tablespoons oil

Combine the orange juice and rice vinegar. Slowly add the liquid to the achiote paste, one tablespoon at a time, while you blend with a fork. You may also use a food processor to blend. While the machine is running, slowly add liquid through the feed tube. Once the liquid and the achiote paste are well blended, add the oregano, cumin seed, salt, pepper, garlic, and oil.

Makes a generous 1 and 1/2 cups salsa. Keeps for 2 months in refrigerator.

PORK ADOBO

This dish deserves to be eaten with black beans and lots of corn tortillas to wrap up the spicy meat.

1 pork shoulder, cut into 2-inch pieces

or 4 pounds country spareribs
2-3 tablespoons light oil
1/2 cup Achiote Salsa
1 can beer, any brand
1 onion, sliced

Brown pork in oil. Remove to side dish while you pour off any excess oil and fat after browning. Pour the achiote over all the meat, making sure that it covers all surfaces.

Place the meat back into the pot, preferably a dutch oven, add the can of beer and place the onion slices on top of the meat Place on a lid or double thickness of foil. Bake at 350 degrees for about 2 hours.

Serves 6.

YUCATECAN BEACH BARBEQUE

The local fisherman and divers off the Mexican Carribean islands of Isla Mujeres and Cozumel are skilled beach chefs at grilling their freshly caught mero, a fish similar to sea bass. One of the best meals of my life was started by a shirtless boy in the back of an old boat anchored off Isla Mujeres. He started with achiote paste, sour oranges, and a green bottle of something that looked like Geni lamp oil. He rubbed his concoction over several butterflied meros laid out on a plank. The planked fish was then carried on his head as he waded through turquoise waters to the beach where his compadres had build a fire of palmetto. Using a grill of green sticks the mero was laid over a slowly dying fire. When the fish was done, it was carried back over the water and we sat on the edge of the boat eating mero with our fingers, chased down by tepid beer.

l whole red snapper or rock cod, butterflied
About l/4 cup Achiote Salsa
l stainless steel hinged grill, in place of green sticks

Rub the salsa on the exposed flesh of the fish. Do not rub on the skin side. Place fish inside the hinged grill (the grill makes it easier to turn the fish) and place over coals covered by white ash. Cook the fish skin side down for l0 minutes and then turn to the side basted with salsa. Grill for about another l0 minutes. Exact timing is dependent on size of fish but most rock cod available weigh about 2 and l/2 pounds so will require no more than 20 minutes total. To test for doneness use a fork to see if the fish will pull away easily from the skin. If it lifts easily, it is done. If you allow it to flake too easily, it is overdone.

Serve the grilled fish with a tossed salad or with a stack of tortillas, chopped tomatoes, limes, salsa, and lettuce and make fish tacos. And if you serve fish tacos, you might as well serve black beans to be really faithful to Yucatecan tradition.

Only serves 4 because it tastes so good.

CHAPTER VI
FRUIT SALSAS

In romantic, tropical places such as the Hawaiian Islands, Polynesian Islands, and the Carribean where fresh fruit is a major part of the diet, the little hot chiles sometimes known as bird peppers and in Tahiti as Tabascos have long been delicately combined with pineapple, mango, and papaya.

To enjoy these fruit salsas, you have to change your old frame of reference from bowls of red and green to bowls filled with colorful fruit speckled with bits of chile and cilantro. These tropic-inspired salsas have whetted the appetites and creativity of West Coast chefs. They are being enjoyed as relishes, rather than dips, alongside grilled fish, chicken, and pork. At first, I resisted because I am very tradition-oriented and I felt the salsas were trendy. Trendy in California but traditional in Tahiti.

I found lethal, tiny hot chiles in the native market in Papeete, Tahiti residing in what looked like green moonshine bottles. When I asked the stall lady how she used the peppers, she smiled and said, "Everything. Eggs. Fruit. Everything." The bottled peppers, obviously of great value, cost as much in Polynesian francs ($16 American dollars) as one small bunch of the prized Tahitian vanilla pods. When packing for the trip back to California, I placed my bottle of costly pickled peppers alongside my French perfume in my carry-on bag and while we were preoccupied saying goodbye to friends at LAX, the bag was stolen. I cursed the thief and hoped he would sear himself with my peppers, the loss of which I cried over more than the loss of the Shalimar.

FRESH PINEAPPLE SALSA

Unwilling to prejudice you entirely, I will simply say that this is one of my favorites. This salsa is perfect with barbecued or grilled chicken or grilled fish. Languish by your barbecue on a hot summer evening and when the coals have gotten past the searing hot stage and are covered by white ash, lay on some boned, pounded chicken breasts. They will be ready in three or four minutes per side. Then warm some bread or tortillas on the same grill and serve pineapple salsa.

Cut off the portion of the pineapple that you need. Trim off the rough peel and dice the fruit.

2 cups fresh pineapple, diced
1/2 cup jicama, peeled and diced
1/3 cup red onion, minced
1/2 cup red bell pepper, diced
1 serrano or jalapeño chile, seeds removed,
*   minced*
2 teaspoons fresh ginger, minced
1/4 to 1/2 teaspoon dried, small chile, crushed
(you can use the japones or arbol chile)
1 tablespoon rice vinegar (not seasoned) or juice

Jicama is the white Mexican root vegetable covered by a brownish skin resembling that of a young Russet potato. It is becoming more available in markets and can be requested. Peel the jicama with a paring knife and dice. Jicama is very bland but absorbs flavors of dressings and spices marvelously and provides an unbeatable crisp texture. If you cannot find jicama, you could get away with canned water chestnuts, diced. I favor using the serrano chile and treat it as do the Mexicans. I mince it, leaving in all the seeds and veins. This makes a little hotter salsa but we like it that way. Add the rest of the ingredients and mix lightly. Taste for seasoning to see if you would like a little more crushed red pepper or cilantro. Keeps nicely for two days in the refrigerator.

Makes about 3 cups pineapple salsa. Serves 4-6 as a relish.

FANTASTIC TAHITIAN CHICKEN SALAD

My husband, Robert, says that he has never in his entire life eaten a better chicken salad and I discovered it by combining leftover pineapple salsa with poached chicken breasts and mayonnaise. The chicken salad is also good in a hollowed out loaf of French bread and some red leaf lettuce for a great sandwich. Or hollow out half of your pineapple with the green stalk intact and stuff it with chicken salad.

1 recipe of the above pineapple salsa
2 whole chicken breasts
2 14 and 1/2 ounce cans chicken broth
1 can water
1 lemon, sliced
1/2 cup to 3/4 cup mayonnaise
1 tablespoon lemon or lime juice
1 teaspoon Dijon mustard
1/4 teaspoon powdered ginger (or more)

Make the pineapple salsa and chill. If you are using up leftover pineapple salsa (if you have about 1 and 1/2 cups left), you can poach just 1 whole chicken breast and combine with less mayonnaise.

Poach the chicken breasts by combining in 3-quart pot with broth, water, and sliced lemon. Bring to simmer and cook on low heat for about 20 minutes and allow to cool in the broth. Remove the chicken and cut off from bone. Dice and add to the pineapple salsa along with the rest of the ingredients. Taste for seasonings. The amount of mayonnaise you use will depend upon how creamy you want your salad or sandwich filling. You could also substitute half plain low-fat or nonfat yogurt if you were concerned about fat content.

Ingredients to play with according to your taste:
fresh ginger, red pepper flakes, powdered ginger,
lime or lemon juice, rice vinegar, cilantro, and
amount of mayonnaise.

PAPAYA SALSA

With papaya and mango, I feel the same way as
with avocado. Do not let them hang around the
kitchen ripening into brownish pap; this is really easy
to do with imported tropical fruits, which sometimes
seem to ripen from the inside out, so upon a gentle
squeeze they appear too firm to use. For fruit salsas,
it is best to use firm, not overly ripe fruits. Salsa
should have texture as opposed to being in a state of
fruity mush.

2 cups of papaya (about one Hawaiian papaya)
1/2 cup red bell pepper, diced
1 serrano or jalapeño chile, minced
1/4 cup red onion, diced
1/2 teaspoon dried red pepper, crushed
Juice from 1 lime
2 tablespoons cilantro, snipped

Once you have diced all the fruit and the accompanying vegetables, very gently stir with the spices and lime juice. I include sweet red bell peppers in most of the fruit salsas because they impart a crisp texture as a foil to the softer fruit. This salsa goes best with grilled fish and keeps well for a day.

Ingredients to play with: minced green onion, red pepper flakes, rice vinegar instead of lime juice, cilantro, and diced fresh pineapple which will add even more texture to the papaya.

TROPICAL SALSA FOR THE AUTUMN

This is one of the most beautiful and least picante of the fruit salsas.   I concocted it during November when pomegrantes and the crisp Japanese persimmons (Fuyu) were in season. For a holiday dinner, I warmed the salsa and served it with a magnificent crown pork roast and wild rice pancakes. It makes a beautiful presentation when served in a crystal dish and is one of those salsas that crosses the line into salads and relishes.

1 cup fresh pineapple, peeled and diced
1 mango, peeled and diced
1 papaya, peeled, seeded, diced
1 Fuyu persimmon, peeled and diced (optional but great)
1 cup jicama, peeled and diced
Seeds from 1 pomegrante (optional but beautiful)
1 cup red onion, diced
1 red bell pepper, seeded and diced
1 serrano or jalapeño chile, seeded and minced
1 dried chipotle chile, seeded and pulverized
1/2 teaspoon powdered ginger
Juice from 1 lime
1 tablespoons rice vinegar
2 tablespoons cilantro, snipped with scissors

This salsa keeps well for 2 days so you can make it the morning of your dinner. After you have diced all the fruits and vegetables, gently stir in the seasonings. You can delete two of the fruit types such as the persimmon or the mango if they are difficult to find but you must try to combine a minimum of three fruits for the excitement of the tastes and textures. The chipotle chile is a dried, smoked jalapeño that has become my obscession since I discovered its power. It provides a hot smokiness that is incomparable. See Sources at the end of the book for how to obtain the dried chipotle. Do not use the canned variety for this fruit salsa although you may substitute a dried chile such as arbol or japonés.

For a barbecue, the tropical salsa is good chilled but for an elegant dinner, the flavors are most pronounced if the salsa is warmed for 3 minutes in a 325 degree oven or briefly in a microwave oven. You want to warm the fruit not cook it.

MANGO SALSA

The heat of the small chile is a perfect foil for the sweetness of the fruit. This salsa, Carribean-style, accompanies grilled fish.

1 mango, diced
1 half of a cantalope
1/2 cup red onion, diced
1/2 teaspoon crushed red pepper
1 serrano chile, seeded, minced
Juice from 2 limes

Dice and mince and very gently mix everything with the fresh lime juice. Keeps well for 1 day.

Ingredients to play with: for textural variation you may add a diced apple or some diced jicama.

MELON SALSA

To enjoy fruit salsas, you have to forget many of your preconceived ideas. I remember how shocked I was to see the fruit vendors in San Miguel de Allende, where I lived for a couple of years, sprinkling salt and ground red chile over chunks of pineapple, papaya, and melon. In Mexican markets you can find bottles of Pico de Gallo (referring in jest to the bite of the rooster's beak) salt. Appropriately, there is a picture of a red and yellow rooster on the label. This special salt is just a mixture of ground red chiles and salt. The bottle instructs you to sprinkle lime juice and Pico de Gallo over fruit, corn, cucumbers, etc. Like most of the fruit salsas, the melon salsa is to be eaten as a relish. It is not as good if the melon is tasteless and the mint must be pungent and minty.

1 ripe cantalope
1 tablespoon fresh mint, cut into slivers
Juice from 1 lime
1 small dried red chile (japonés, arbol, or pequín)
Pinch of salt (optional)

Dice the cantalope and sprinkle with mint, lime juice, and red chile which you have crushed. A pinch of salt will bring out the flavors of the melon. Serve melon salsa to accompany barbecued meats or grilled fish.

CRANBERRY SALSA

Of course, this is made for chicken and turkey but yesterday I found my husband eating it out of the bowl in front of the open refrigerator. People who are not mad about cranberry sauce will go wild over this salsa. What makes it fun is that it is not what people are expecting. Since I am always trying to invent the Great Sandwich, I have already successfully married this salsa to a turkey on whole wheat.

147

4 cups of fresh or frozen cranberries
1/2 cup red onion, chopped
Juice of 1 lime
1/2 cup orange juice
2 small dried red chiles, japonés or serrano, crushed
1 jalapeño or serrano chile, minced
1/2 cup brown sugar
2 tablespoons honey

Using a food processor, chop cranberries coarsely .
Toward the end of processing, add the onion and
chop. Then simmer everything together for 10 minutes. Do not overcook to retain good texture.
The salsa will become a brilliant red.
My tester ate every bite.   When I needed to test this
salsa, spring was almost here and I went everywhere
hopelessly looking for cranberries. Finally, I assumed the recipe would have to be left out of the
book. We had to make a trip to San Jose in Northern
California and we discovered a grocery store called
Cosentino's with beautiful vegetables-there were
bunches of fresh field lettuces, sorrel, Italian parsley,
basil, tiny Blue Lake green beans, and cranberries out
of season. Cosentino's started out 30 years ago as a
vegetable stand and is still run by the same family.

CHAPTER VII

SALSA TECHNIQUES

One of the most frequent questions I get asked is, "What is the best way to make salsa? And the answer is there is no pat answer. Ultimately, it depends upon whether you are working with a sharp knife or a rusty one; whether you have tomatoes bred sweetly or industrially; or whether you are one of those cooks who want to plunge into the ingredients HANDS ON or whether you want to process them quickly into a salsa. Sometimes, like you, I feel like all my knives are dull, my tomatoes belong to science, and I'm tired. In that case, I put some canned tomatoes (usually of the Italian pomidoro kind) into my faithful food processor. Add the rest of the chosen ingredients of the salsa and chop. I don't even feel guilty and neither should you.

HAND AND KNIFE TECHNIQUE

This is my favorite technique when my tomatoes are real, particularly in the summer and autumn. Then I make sure that my favorite 10-inch knife is sharp. I don't even peel the tomatoes but just cut them in half horizontally and while holding them over the sink, squeeze out most of the seeds and some excess juice. I dice them and add the rest of the ingredients such as with the recipes for Pico de Gallo (page 15) and Salsa Cruda (page 19). In Mexico, anytime you fix a fresh, chopped salsa it is called salsa cruda (literally raw sauce). If you have a well-sharpened chef's knife, this is one of the fastest salsas you can make. The hand and knife technique will reward you with the unadulterated, unwhizzed taste of pure, sweet tomatoes and you will probably acquire a halo equivalent to the aura that surrounds you when you are kneading bread dough.

One of the very best of the salsa crudas that I have tasted is the one prepared at the Parkway Grill in Pasadena. The chef calls his version salsa de cerveza, meaning beer salsa. This is how it goes: in the morning, he chops up some fantastic tomatoes, he adds a few minced serrano chiles with the seeds included, some minced red onion, a couple of cloves

of garlic, some fresh cilantro and a dash of balsamic vinegar and a dash of champagne vinegar.
Now for the secret ingredient. He adds a few tablespoons of beer and that is it. When I asked what kind of beer, the waitress looked amazed and replied, "Whatever kind of beer he is drinking that morning!" As a finishing touch, I drizzle in a few teaspoons of good olive oil. There can be no exacting recipe for Salsa de Cerveza because you must work from inspiration, good ingredients and start out with small amounts of some things like the chile and cilantro (and beer) and keep adding until you like the taste.
 I use a lighter beer because I don't want the beer flavor to take over the salsa.   Do not make this in the food processor.

FOOD PROCESSOR TECHNIQUE

When I am working with roasted tomatoes such as in the recipe for Blackened Salsa (page 43), the food processor does a perfect job. By using short on and off pulsations, you can chop everything together - the tomatoes, garlic, onions, and chiles. Done in the processor, the salsa becomes a marvelous roasted red color with just the right amount of threatening black flecks. You can also use a blender but it would tend to puree more than chop. The blender and the food processor seem to work best with tomatoes which have been either briefly cooked or roasted or cooked completely. If you are using canned tomatoes such as with the Santa Maria Salsa (page 28), the food processor does a great job of making salsa. As stated earlier in this book, raw tomatoes, which have more water, tend to become aerated and pink when you attempt to chop them in a food processor or blender. Process with short, quick pulses and add a couple of tablespoons of olive oil and canned tomato sauce to discourage the bubbling effect.

The most propitious time to rely on food processors is either when you are in a hurry or you are working with roasted, partially cooked, or canned tomatoes.

MINI-WHISK TECHNIQUE

The automatic whisk, resembling a power drill, is a great gadget for sticking into a bowl of salsa or sauce and chopping it into a rough puree.
Restaurant chefs have giant versions of these automatic whisks (or blenders on a stick) which is the only safe way that they can puree large batches of soup and sauces. Their greatest advantage is that the tool is plunged directly into the salsa, allowing you to chop or puree a small portion at a time with less of a chance of overprocessing.

It also works best with cooked ingredients. I originally bought it for whipping my Spanish chocolate into a froth (instead of using a molinillo) and for pureeing split pea soup right in the pot after I had gotten burned from trying to splash hot pea soup into the blender jar. The brand I have is made by Braun and is also known as a miniprimer.

COOKING THE SALSA

Sometimes a salsa can have an unfinished or raw taste even though you have combined all the ingredients called for and you just don't know what more to add. This minor occurrence is often due to tomatoes which have been artificially ripened or are not ripe enough, or perhaps have a lot of acid. Just place the salsa in an open skillet and simmer for as little as five minutes. The simmering seems to bring out the flavors of the tomatoes and can transform an unexciting salsa into a wonderful one.

MICROWAVING TOMATILLOS
(NEW DISCOVERY)

If I am trying to reduce the liquid in a salsa in order to concentrate the flavors, I still prefer simmering the ingredients in an open skillet.

But the microwave oven is the best answer yet for cooking the Mexican tomatillos, the little green tomatoes covered with a papery husk, which are the basis for green salsas. I have a small microwave oven that in the past has just been used for heating milk, melting butter and chocolate, and warming leftovers. It does a perfect job of cooking the tomatillos as opposed to the traditional way of roasting them, with their husks still intact, in a hot skillet. The microwaved tomatillos are better in flavor, tasting fresher, and stay a beautiful bright green. This innovative technique was suggested to me by one of my readers who said she didn't have a lot of time. Your salsa will never have that greyish-green color of overcooked tomatillos. If you have a food processor to chop the salsa, you will be able to have tomatillo sauce in five minutes.

Wash off in warm water and remove papery husks from one and a half pounds of tomatillos. Place in single layer on a dinner plate or flat microwave dish. Microwave on full power for 2 minutes (for a small 500 watt oven). Remove and chop in a food processor, adding the rest of the required ingredients (see pages 23 and 39 for recipes). You will love the fresh, bright flavor.

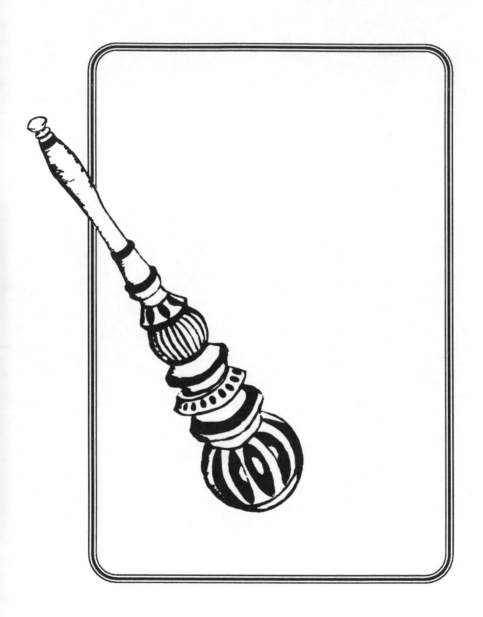

156

CHAPTER VIII
CHOCOLATE ENDINGS AND CHOCOLATE FOR BREAKFAST

At the conclusion of a *picante* meal or an over-dose of salsa, there is nothing more soothing than chocolate in some form. Chocolate tranquilizes the shock to the palate, brought on by too much capsa-icin.

The ancients of Mexico long ago discovered this trait of chocolate but it was reserved for use only by priests and nobles. The supreme epicure, Mon-tezuma, was the first to discover the pleasures of chocolate ice cream, sending his runners to the tops of snow-capped volcanoes to collect blocks of ice over which thick, hot chocolate was poured, beaten, and whipped into Aztec ice cream.

ONE-PAN BROWNIES

After serving guests, platters of my Latin or Cali-fornia Rancho dishes and an array of spicy salsas, I like to soothe them with small portions of warm, thick brownies swathed in Mexican Chocolate Sauce. No one has ever been ungrateful for this chocolate ending which I could call "the chile tranquilizer."

2 squares unsweetened chocolate
l stick butter
l/2 cup brown sugar
l/2 cup white sugar
2 tablespoons honey
2 eggs
3/4 cup all-purpose flour
l/4 teaspoon baking powder
l tablespoon vanilla
2 cups chopped nuts

In a 2-quart saucepan, melt the chocolate and butter together, stirring in the brown and white sugar when everything is just about melted. Keep stirring. After the chocolate and butters have melted and the sugars are blended, remove from heat and stir in the honey. Allow the mixture to cool down for a couple of minutes before beating in the eggs one at a time. Next stir in the flour, baking powder, vanilla, and nuts.

Pour into a greased, square 8-inch pan. Bake in a preheated 350 degree oven for about 30 minutes or until a toothpick comes out clean or just a thin film of chocolate clings to the tester. You do not want the brownies too fudgey because you are going to serve them with chocolate sauce.

Serves 8.

SALSA DE CHOCOLATE MEXICANA

This chocolate sauce was inspired both by Maida Heatter and by a sauce eaten in a Mexican hacienda where the chocolate had been ground by hand on a metate. I admired the chocolate so much that when I left I was given two imperfect, molded rounds of grainy chocolate wrapped in blue and pink tissue paper. As a third deadly sin, I like to add powdered expresso powder, a little powdered sugar, and vanilla to softly whipped cream and put that on top of the warm chocolate sauce and warm brownies. Salsa de Chocolate Mexicana is also great over ice cream.

3/4 cup evaporated milk or cream
1 tablet of Mexican chocolate (Ibarra), 3.1 ounces
A healthy pinch cinnamon
3 tablespoons sweet butter
1/4 cup sugar
1/4 cup brown sugar
1/3 cup unsweetened cocoa powder

Chop up the Mexican chocolate and add it to a 2-quart saucepan containing the evaporated milk, cinnamon, and sweet butter. You may substitute another sweet chocolate for the Mexican brand. The Mexican chocolate is grainy so stir the melting chocolate and milk mixture with a whisk until all is well blended. Next stir in the sugars and cocoa powder, continuing to gently blend with a whisk. Keep stirring over low heat so sugars and cocoa are dissolved.

The sauce stores well refrigerated but will thicken. Thin it out with more evaporated milk or cream. Warm the sauce before serving.

8 servings to normal dessert eaters.
4 servings to chocolate addicts.

VELVET HOT CHOCOLATE FROM RANCHO DAYS

As a tradition from the early days of California, thick, hot chocolate was served on our rancho. It was especially favored for breakfast, being a perfect foil for *picante* huevos rancheros but it was also taken in the evening with rolls. Even Brillat-Savarin stated, "Every spiritual man who feels bestiality growing within him again, every man who feels his surroundings are difficult to overcome, must drink a pint of perfumed chocolate and everything will seem marvelous!"

This chocolate was traditionally whipped into a froth with a wooden molinillo but you may use a wire whisk or electric whisk.

4 squares semi-sweet chocolate, chopped
l cup boiling water

4 cups milk
l cup cream
2-3 tablespoons sugar
l teaspoon vanilla
l/4 teaspoon cinnamon
Pinch of allspice and nutmeg
2 eggs, beaten

Whisk the chocolate and the hot water together until well dissolved in a 2-quart saucepan over medium heat. While you gently whisk, add the milk, cream, sugar, vanilla, cinnamon, nutmeg, and allspice. Drizzle in the beaten eggs slowly blending them well into the milk mixture. After 15 minutes of slow simmering over a medium heat, the hot chocolate will thicken enough to coat a spoon.

In order to serve the chocolate in the traditional way, it is best to pour the chocolate into a high pitcher so it can be whipped into a froth. If you do this in a saucepan, you are likely to splatter yourself and the entire kitchen. Hold the wire whisk or wooden molinillo, the Indian utensil used for beating chocolate, between the palms of your hands. Place the whisk into the pitcher of hot chocolate and twirl it back and forth between your palms. If you hold the beater a little above the surface of the liquid you will create even more aeration.

Hold an upside down spoon over each cup and pour the chocolate over the spoon and into the cup. If done this way, you will not deflate the chocolate and each cup will have a cap of chocolate bubbles

A cup of this foaming chocolate elixir would save Brillat-Savarin from the doldrums.

Serves 8 small cups.

CHAMPURRADO

Champurrado, traditionally in Mexico and the Southwest, is a chocolate-flavored gruel thickened with masa or treated cornmeal. If you grew up on traditional champurrado, you probably love it like some people love sticky oatmeal.

Our champurrado here is nontraditional, non-nursery food, and reminiscent of the thick hot chocolate served in the cafes of Spain, making it very close to the drink served in Old California when chocolate was the only beverage available except for an occasional whiskey.

2 ounces semi-sweet chocolate, chopped
3/4 cup hot water
1 quart of whole milk, heated
3 tablespoons sugar
1/2 of a vanilla bean, split
2 eggs, beaten
1 tablespoon plus 1 teaspoon cornstarch
Cinnamon sticks to place in each cup (optional)

Pour the hot water over the chocolate and stir, until melted, over medium heat. Then add the heated milk, sugar, and vanilla bean. Slowly whisk in the beaten eggs. In a small bowl, stir some of the milk mixture into the cornstarch, making sure it is well-dissolved. Whisk the milk-cornstarch into the chocolate liquid, blending it together. After simmering over a medium heat for about 10 minutes, the chocolate will thickly coat a spoon. Pour it into cups and serve warm, not hot.

Serves 6-8 as a breakfast drink or for the traditional holiday repast along with sweet tamales.

INDEX

164

165

SOURCES

WHERE YOU CAN FIND CHILES AND OTHER SOUTHWESTERN INGREDIENTS

THE GREEN CHILI FIX CO. OF SANTA FE
P.O. Box 5463, Santa Fe, New Mexico 87502.
505-471-3325.

Have wonderful dried green chile, sold in whole pieces or ground. Can be reconstituted or sprinkled as a seasoning. This is the next best thing to having fresh New Mexican chiles. Also carry chipotles, the smoked, dried jalapeños.

THE CHILE SHOP
109 E. Water St. , Santa Fe, New Mexico 87501
505-983-6080.

Sueanne and Ted have my favorite chile powders, the Dixon and the Chimayo, and the mild Hatch ground chile for gringos along with a good selection of blue cornmeal in all its guises, ristras, and all kinds of Southwestern cooking ingredients. Have a catalog and are happy to mail order or answer inquiries by phone.

PEPPERS
4009 N. Brown Ave.Scottsdale, Arizona 85251
602-990-8347

Peppers has grown to four stores and they are all run by the same Basque family. They mail order beautiful fresh ristras of the Sandia chile, ristras of the hot pequin chile that is so good in fruit salsas, ancho chile pods, and they have available several chile products such as jams, salsas, and jellies. Have catalog and do phone orders.

PEPPERS OF OLD TOWN
328 San Felipe Rd. N.W.
Albuquerque, NM 87104
505-242-7538

Peppers has a lot of their own products such as jams, pico de gallo, salsas, and they put together Care packages from New Mexico along with dried chile pods and ristras from the area. I would much rather have one of their Care packages than chocolates. They also stock the marvelous Anazazi beans.

OTHER PLACES FOR CHILES

You have to seek out the stores where the natives shop. It could be a fruit and vegetable stand along the road. In New Mexico and Arizona, during the real chile season from the end of July to October-November, you will find roadside stands and farms advertising chile—even roasted chiles. Wherever I am traveling, I head for the marketplace, the more native the better. But when I am at home in Southern California, I drive into Los Angeles to obtain the hard-to-find chiles such as the chipotles.

My favorite place is the old Grand Central Market on 3rd and Hill; they have everthing and I have frequently seen restaurant chefs tracking down unusual ingredients there. Produce is piled in attractive mounds but the vendors will not let you pick out your own stuff. They will give you a rotten tomato occasionally (that is part of the game) so look in your bag and if you see something suspicious lurking within, hand it back with a smile and ask for another. If you argue, you may get an argument back and you can't win but I love the raucousness of it all. The dark aisles piled with produce. The strange tongues spoken at every stall and I miss the gentle Greek man with his long white apron and aristocratic nose. His sweet butter was the best. I have never found El Mercado, the large, three-tiered Mexican marketplace in East L.A., to have as good a selection as Grand Central. Besides, I don't like getting my tires punctured while I am looking for chiles.

At Tianguis, 1201 W. Whittier Blvd., Montebello, California you have a prettified, modern version of a Grand Central-type market. They have 400 types of fruits and vegetables, a car-nicería with all of the Mexican cuts of meat and more kinds of chorizo than I've ever seen. Their panadería has the best telera rolls I've ever eaten and there is a tortilla factory right on the premises.

In the Mission district of San Francisco, you could spend the day eating and finding cooking ingredients. Raul Barraza of "B" Productos Mexicanos at 2840 Mission St. carries mas o menos 25 types of chiles. This is a great stop if you need chiles for mole poblano. He also carries more Mexican chocolate types than I've seen anywhere.

CHILE SEEDS

Horticultural Enterprises
P.O. Box 340082, Dallas, Texas 75234

They carry all of the Mexican and South American varieties of seeds as well as the seeds for epazote, the herb needed for seasoning black beans and tortilla soup.

Shepherd's Garden Seeds
7389 West Zayante, Felton, California 95018
408-335-5400

Have a great selection of herb seeds and chile seeds all the way from the mild Anaheim to the poblano/anchos.

COOKING SCHOOLS

SANTA FE SCHOOL OF COOKING AND MARKET
Plaza Mercado - 116 W. San Francisco St.
Santa Fe, New Mexico 87501
505-983-4511

Daily classes in traditional New Mexico cooking. Carry a wide assortment of native ingredients, New Mexican herbs and spices, such as the hard-to-find epazote, in the dried form. They will ship.